What Young India Wants

CHETAN BHAGAT is the author of five novels, all of which have gone on to become blockbuster sellers since they were released. They have also been adapted into major Bollywood films. In addition to being a bestselling author, Chetan is a motivational speaker and columnist. He was named one of the '100 Most Influential People in the World' by *Time* magazine and one of the world's '100 Most Creative People in Business' by Fast Company, USA.

He lives in Mumbai with his wife Anusha, an ex-classmate from IIM-A, and his twin boys Shyam and Ishaan.

You can get in touch with Chetan on Twitter (@chetan_ bhagat) and Facebook (facebook.com/chetanbhagat. fanpage). You can also visit www.chetanbhagat.com or email him at info@chetanbhagat.com.

WHAT YOUNG INDIA WANTS

Selected Essays and Columns

Chetan Bhagat

RUPA

Published by
Rupa Publications India Pvt. Ltd 2012
7/16, Ansari Road, Daryaganj
New Delhi 110002

Sales centres:
Allahabad Bengaluru Chennai
Hyderabad Jaipur Kathmandu
Kolkata Mumbai

ISBN: 978-81-291-2021-2

10 9 8

The moral right of the author has been asserted.

Printed at Nutech Print Services, Faridabad

Contents

OUR YOUTH

TWO STORIES

My Journey

Dear Reader,

Thank you for picking up this book. This is not a novel. This is my first non-fiction compilation—a collection of my thoughts about various issues facing India in the past two years. I have felt equal passion writing these chapters as I feel while writing an emotional story. I have written them in various states of mind—anger, anguish, frustration, sadness or hope. In these pages you will find not only the India of now, but also the India of my dreams. And read together, I hope that from this you will get an overview of what India is today, and what India can be.

Why This Letter

Why do I write about national issues? Why should a popular fiction novelist comment on society and current events? What right do I have to think that I can and should give my take on issues facing the country? After all, I write stories about young people making out in confined spaces, or drinking vodka on the terrace, or falling in love. How can I write about corruption, elections, political parties, economics and social challenges? Can a person who works with Bollywood filmmakers ever be a meaningful voice on the nation's burning issues? The purpose of this letter is to provide answers to some of these questions as well.

The chapters that make up this book didn't just happen. These were a part of my destiny, especially when I look back at my life and see what shaped my views. For this, you need to understand my background and my relationship with India, a country that has given me so much. Let me take you on a quick tour of my life so far.

Childhood

I come from a simple middle-class family. Both my parents worked for the government and I grew up in Delhi. Throughout my childhood, I remember the shortage of money being a constant theme in the house. We had enough to run the kitchen and pay for utilities but little to build assets on or make major expenses. For instance, we couldn't repair a broken sofa for years. When guests came to our house, we found it expensive to serve Coke and served lemonade instead. We rarely ate out in restaurants and when we did, we did so with caution, figuring out the cheapest and most-filling items on the menu.

Funnily enough, we never felt deprived. I took the shortage of money as an essential factor of life. In a country like India, we were still better off than millions. All I wanted was a decent job when I grew up and enough money so that it wasn't a constant problem.

I liked science subjects, and was told engineers get guaranteed jobs. I also liked entertaining people. Since childhood, my uncles and aunts used to ask me to tell jokes at parties. I enjoyed this, but nobody ever took it seriously. What was the point of entertaining people anyway? I was told to focus on science and prepare for entrance exams. And that is what I did.

College

I prepared for the IIT exams, aiming high and hoping to at least make it to a medium-ranked college. I studied for two years, though in a somewhat haphazard manner, using Xeroxed notes and all sorts of texts ranging from Russian physics books to correspondence class materials. Nobody in my family had ever made it to an IIT. Nobody expected me to either.

However, with a stroke of luck, I made it. I even achieved a decent rank. I joined Mechanical Engineering at IIT Delhi, and that became a turning point of my life. I joined in 1991, which was also a turning point for India given the economic reforms. IIT did for me what liberalization did for India—created opportunities and changed me forever.

I was never an extraordinary student at IIT. It had some

real geniuses and I was not one of them. While many IITians figured out machines, I realized something else. I was more interested in people. I observed all the students at IIT. They came from all parts of India, toppers in their respective schools. Few had come there to research science or learn about technology. Most had come to achieve their middle-class dream—a better life. And that is what the IITs promised them.

The interest in people made me join IIM-A to do an MBA. I did far better in my MBA course than engineering and ended up near the top of the class. After completing my course, I joined a Hong Kong-based investment bank called Peregrine. I had never been out of India and the chance to go abroad was too exciting a prospect. The money was good. I also wanted to see China develop. Hong Kong gave me a chance to do that.

Hong Kong and My Economics Lessons

Hong Kong opened my eyes as soon as I landed in the city. I had never imagined, let alone visited, a place so developed and affluent. The roads were smooth, the streets were clean and the buildings slick. There were no poor people visible. Public transport was better than private transport, unlike in India. I spent my first few weeks in Hong Kong in shock. How could a place be so well run? How had that society figured it out? And eventually, the questions came—why isn't India like this? Why are we so poor?

Ever since childhood, we are told that India is a great country. Our past political leaders are shown as icons and heroes. We celebrate their birthdays as if they have done wonders for India. We never question them. Did they take the best decisions for us? Were they honest and capable?

I was also told all my life that the Indian people and our culture is wonderful. As a child, I was supposed to be proud of everything Indian. Now all those beliefs lay shattered.

Questions started popping in my head at regular intervals. Why are we one of the poorest nations on earth? Why do we have all sorts of social ills? Why are we so divided, so oppressive, so unfair and so corrupt?

Hong Kong stoked my desire to understand nations and economies better. I feel everyone who has a chance should step out of India for a while to really see what it is like out there. My job in the investment bank gave me a chance to see how money flows around the world. And I could see that India didn't matter. Even though in India we had all sorts of statistics supporting our greatness, foreign investors cared little for India (this was in the late nineties. India is somewhat more important now).

In some ways, Hong Kong shook me up. I was no longer someone who went to great colleges in a great country. I came from a poor, irrelevant country. Period. The world was much richer, smarter, fairer and, from what

I could tell, happier. All our spirituality, diverse cultural identities, policies had brought us nowhere.

The Guilt

Meanwhile, I prospered. I did reasonably well in the bank. There were some hiccups. The bank I started my career at, Peregrine, collapsed in the Asian crisis of 1997. I spent a few jobless months in expensive Hong Kong, but ended up in Goldman Sachs, one of the leading investment banks of the world.

At Goldman, I joined the ratings advisory department. Along with my seniors, we guided the governments of Thailand, Malaysia and Philippines on how to improve their credit ratings. We also helped them liaise with the strict international rating agencies. It was a tough assignment, but one of the most exciting jobs I have ever had. We met finance ministers, rating agency heads and economists. I pored over government data and tried to make sense of it. It was there that I learnt a lot about a nation's economy. I spent months in Thailand and Philippines, working with the government as they handled a balance-of-payments crisis. Because of that exposure, I became well-versed in economics. I found a different approach among politicians in these countries. Sure, they were politicians and prone to people-pleasing tactics, even at the expense of the nation. However, they took economic growth and foreign investment seriously.

All Far East Asian countries have been transformed by foreign investment. The politicians realize the potential of international capital coming into the nation. Finance ministers in these countries lobby with Silicon Valley companies to set up factories in their country, something that is unthinkable in India. Foreign investors need a level playing field, free and fair markets, ease of running a business and the government's commitment towards creating world-class infrastructure. They also need a transparent and strong legal system. These requirements are good for the citizens of the nation anyway. Hence, foreign investors, if brought in well, can help in the nation's development. The Indian government wants foreign investment but ignore the basic expectations that come with it. Hence we receive a fraction of the foreign direct investment compared to some of the Asian economies. In Far East Asian countries, politicians play dirty politics too. However, they don't mess with business.

For a while, I was full of ideas and enthusiasm on what India can do. 'Open the economy'; 'Attract investment'; 'Make the environment business friendly' became my buzzwords.

Sure, these were all great thoughts. However, they were also naïve. I knew the solutions but I didn't know why India couldn't implement them. I also didn't have the means or the way to convince my country—both the common people and the policymakers—that we were on the wrong path. I wanted to scream from the rooftops, 'We will lose the race to these nations if we don't focus!' However, I had no way to do it.

Despite all the love and optimism for my country, a sense of cynicism and frustration had set in. I became the typical armchair NRI advisor. Whenever I heard about bad policies created by Indian politicians, I became depressed. Every time there was news about communal or regional violence, I was in pain. 'What the hell were we doing?' I used to ask at NRI parties. 'The finance minister of Malaysia went to meet Intel and lobbied for a chip plant near Kuala Lumpur. Our politicians fought with each other or planned scams!'

'Forget it, this is India. It will never change,' my friends told me.

Sure, I could and should have forgotten about it. We had a good life. We had worked for several years. We had enough money in the bank, air-conditioned homes and an investment-banker lifestyle that allowed us to travel the world in luxury. People gave us further advice, 'Focus on yourself. Anyone who is smart gets out of that messed up country.'

However, I couldn't forget about it. I don't know why, I just couldn't disconnect myself from India. Not a day passed when I didn't keep track of what was happening in India. I was the confused soul who liked the riches of Hong Kong but yearned to make India a better place—without knowing how.

I felt guilt at having so much. I moved into the posh mid-levels area of Hong Kong, where annual rents are more than the price of an apartment in New Delhi. I travelled to a new Asian capital every week, flying business class and staying in style. We had $100 per meal allowances in the finest hotels, even as people in my country found it difficult to get a job for that amount every month. I had a good life mainly because of the degrees I had earned in my own country and I wanted to do something in return. I never thought I could get a chance to do so. After all, this was 2001 and I didn't know what life had in store for me.

Destiny: From Banker to Author

Indians believe in destiny. Some call it luck. Whatever you call it, my life had a plan written for it. Little did I know that I would be able to communicate my ideas for a better India not only to a few but to millions around the country.

I was meant to be a banker, stay a banker. I was an NRI, someone who earns in dollars and spends his evenings being nostalgic about India. I had no idea I would quit banking and be back on the streets of Mumbai. If there is someone who should believe in destiny, it is I.

All of this became possible because of the one little, ignored aspect of my personality when I was a child—me as the entertainer. It surfaced again and changed my life. I mentioned earlier how I used to entertain my uncles and relatives when I was a child. That same entertainer re-emerged in Hong Kong. My other banker friends took on hobbies like golf and bridge. Almost by chance, I decided to do what I enjoyed: tell stories. Perhaps I wanted to get over my depression and frustration. Maybe I wanted to reconnect with India. Whatever the reason, I decided to write a book.

The Books

Everyone found the title of my first book odd. It took me a minute to explain it to people. It referred to grade point averages of the three students in IIT, whom the story was about. Many found the entire book odd. I don't want to go into the heroic story of how I struggled to become an author. Let's just say it wasn't easy. *Five Point Someone* released in May 2004. The book did well and gave me a readership.

I continued to write more books, taking on social issues in each of them. The second book, *One Night@ the Call Center* took on the plight of the call center generation. The third book was a story about secularism set in modern Gujarat, *The 3 Mistakes of My Life*. The readership continued to grow and reached hundreds of thousands.

The books gave me an outlet to express my thoughts about India. However, for the most part, they were entertainers. I could take on a social issue, but each book took two years to write. There was far too much going on in the country that needed comment.

Quitting the Job

After the three books became hits, I started to question myself again. I had a big readership; people had accepted my style of writing; I had a fan base, if you can call it that, of regular readers who trusted me and read my work. I asked myself —could I not do more with this? I had for years wanted to create more awareness for a better India. Wasn't now the time to do it with full gusto?

However, to put in my hundred per cent, I had to quit my lucrative job. As an executive director in a major international investment bank, I had several perks and a big salary. To give it all up and write, hoping to effect change in a country like India, sounded mad from the start. However, I knew that without a streak of madness I would never do this. The golden handcuffs of the bank were hard to get rid of.

I deliberated for over two years. I realized I may fail in my mission if I quit and regret my decision to leave. However, I also realized if I didn't leave, I would regret not trying. Hence, at age thirty-four, I retired. Yes, I emailed my resignation, cleaned up my cubicle and came home.

My wife continued to work. I stayed at home. The first few weeks were difficult—full of anxiety, loneliness and nothing to do. I had only a vague idea of what I would do with the rest of my life.

I started another book, *2 States*, on inter-community marriages. It worked. It became a bigger hit than all previous books. *3 Idiots*, a film based on *Five Point Someone*, released a few months later. It became the highest grossing film in Bollywood history.

Motivational Speaker

Somewhere during this period, a talk titled 'Sparks' at an educational institute became a hit on the Internet. It went viral and launched a new career for me. I became a speaker and attended over a hundred events in more than seventy-five cities, ranging from Amravati to New York, Gorakhpur to Kochi and Guwahati to Jaipur. I learnt more about India and its youth. I realized that even though the regional cultures were different, all Indians wanted the same thing—a better life in a good society. My travels around the country refreshed my understanding. I was no longer an NRI in Hong Kong who commented on India. I was an Indian who spent more than half his time in the heartland interacting with the youth. My stage had become bigger, the audience wider. The time had come to tell whosoever I could reach how we ought to change the nation. And just as destiny had planned it, I received an offer to write columns.

Writing Newspaper Columns

In mid-2008, the Hindi newspaper *Dainik Bhaskar*, which knew of my presence among youth in the heartland, approached me to write for them. An English language author in India writing in Hindi was unthinkable. English had to be elitist, and authors especially so. However, I was intrigued. I asked them if I could write about anything. They replied in the affirmative.

Dainik Bhaskar has a readership in crores. Destiny stood at my door. All my years in Hong Kong learning about economies, my books that had given me a readership, and my talks throughout India that had given me an understanding of my country could now be put to good use. The Hindi audience gave me a chance to reach the majority, the real India. I jumped at the opportunity.

In a few months, destiny gave me another opportunity. I had another offer from *The Times of India*, the biggest English-language newspaper in the country (and even the world). Every two weeks, a combined readership of four crore Indians had access to my writings. Of course, critics asked what a novelist was doing on the serious editorial page. After all, I was no intellectual with grey hair. I couldn't answer them. They were probably right at some level. However, this was destiny. This was meant to happen.

Rocking the Boat

I met Joydeep Bose, the editorial head for *The Times of India*. I took tips from him about writing. I also told him, 'I am here to rock the boat.'

He thought about it for a few seconds and then said, 'Good, that is what we want.'

I started easy, writing columns analyzing the budget, or commenting on simple policies in defence or agriculture. When I look back, those columns carried less heat. Perhaps I was nervous to fully express myself at the start. Perhaps there wasn't so much to get aggressive about.

Then, the Commonwealth Games were held in India in 2010 and it provided a turning point for me. It was also the turning point for many Indians on how they look at our faulty system. The Commonwealth Games scam was easily one of the biggest scams in independent India's history. Yet, the government in its smug arrogance pretended as if nothing had happened. It was then that I took a big risk. I wrote an essay for *The Times of India* in which I asked people to boycott the Commonwealth Games. I wrote it in a state of anger, and the passion showed. The newspaper, huge respect to them, carried it without changing a word. My anger connected with the readers. The essay went viral on the Internet and in many ways established me as a writer of non-fiction. I wouldn't say the column alone led to the intense scrutiny on the games going forward. However, it was one of the early pieces reacting strongly to the scam.

Corruption: My Big Muse

Corruption, and all aspects related to removing it, then became my muse. When the Anna movement started, I tried my best to mobilize youth through my writings as well as the social network. It was obvious—let alone the morality of it; without reducing corruption, we could never hope to become a rich country. Yes, we need new laws like the Lokpal. Yes, the politicians should take a big part of the blame. However, this alone is not going to be enough to end corruption.

What Indians need to understand is that corruption didn't just start and end with politicians. We ourselves are also to blame for it. We have a warped set of values that allows so much graft to take place. We think cheating, in reasonable amounts, is okay. These are not good values. Thus, we as people need to take some responsibility too. Only then true change shall happen.

Corruption is a way of life in India. It is a by-product of a system that is power driven. Our society respects power, not excellence or integrity. Power-driven systems resemble the jungle. The lion is always right and the lion's friends have a good life. Everyone else's place in life is dependent on their power. Sure, such societies can function. However, they don't progress much.

Societies that value excellence, innovation, entrepreneurship and integrity do well. If we want India to be rich, we have to value excellence and honesty first. This is where a reset, a re-prioritization of something very core to society is required. This core is our values.

How Can We Change?

Yes, honesty pays but only if all of society is honest. If only you are honest, but everyone else is not, you will suffer. This is the bottleneck obstructing change in India today. We all want to be honest, but we don't want to be the only one honest, for then we will suffer. This paradox prevents change.

For example, suppose that a crowd of people is waiting for a bus at a stop. When the bus arrives, everybody pushes and shoves to get in. It makes life difficult for everyone. The solution to this daily misery would be everyone queueing up to get in. However, everyone needs to come on board with the queuing system. If you are the only one queuing up, while the others continue to rush in, you will be left behind.

Thus, transformation will come about only if everyone decides to change together. A majority of Indians have to accept what we do is wrong and be ready to change for a better future. Society needs to reset and inculcate good values. Right now, we don't even have a clear set of Indian values. We need to create them. How will all this happen and that too at the same time? Well, this is where leaders come in.

A leader is a human being who can reach a large part of the population. If the leader is charismatic and influential, he or she can create a lot of positive change in people's thinking. If we are lucky enough to have good leaders at the top, change will happen quickly. Unfortunately, we don't. Given how divided India is, how corruption is accepted and how we lack good values, it is impossible for us to choose a good leader at this point.

Deep down we all are skeptical and ashamed of ourselves. Thus, anyone who even tries to change India for the better is seen with cynical eyes. We know we are all tarnished, so we doubt everyone else too. It is a sad situation, where we need a leader but cannot really trust anyone. Anti-corruption protestors are often doubted. I can bet some people reading this will be asking—what is Chetan's agenda? What is he trying to achieve? Who is he trying to please? What does he want? In fact, a leader would be left explaining himself or herself rather than doing any work.

In this chaos, I feel there is a role for artists. What we lack in leaders can be made up to a certain extent by art and artists. Movies, books, music—popular art forms can inject people with modern messages and a new set of Indian values. As a writer with reach, I can at least attempt to present an alternative way of thinking. Sure,

I have no authority as a leader or as much power as an official head. Yet, I have some qualities today what even a senior politician may not have. I have the benefit of being neutral. I am not aligned to any political party, therefore, the cynicism is also reduced. I also have no political aspirations in the foreseeable future, so that reduces doubt about my selfish interests. I make enough money as a motivational speaker and I am not dependent on political patronage. This credibility is priceless in today's times. That, combined with reach, can make a significant impact on public opinion. And that is where, I think, my writings can be most influential.

Have I Made a Difference?

I have a long way to go as a thinker, opinion-maker and writer. The last three years have been a fun learning experience. I have been fortunate enough to make many new acquaintances and friends, many in the corridors of power. These friendships are not for any purpose other than mutual exchange of ideas and understanding each other better. And unless I understand politicians, I cannot propose practical solutions, something extremely important to me. Unless the politicians hear what I am trying to say, which is usually what the youth feels and wants, change will never happen. Across parties, I have met several MPs and ministers in the past two years and tried to explain my thoughts to them.

For reasons of confidentiality, I cannot reveal each and every detail of my meetings. However, here are a few examples:

- A central government minister called me to discuss issues with Air India after I wrote harshly about the airline. He explained his side of the story and promised to take a tough stance. He took a firm position when the airline went on strike.

- The leader of a major political party quoted a piece I'd written about the prime minister at a political rally.

- My writings on the Lokpal Bill gave me a chance to meet members of the civil society and the government to try and bring about some consensus.

- A senior minister of the BJP called me and wrote a detailed letter commenting on the issues I had raised about the party.

- The IAS community congratulated me and circulated an essay I wrote on the need for our babus to have more guts.

I don't want to give more examples. I was hesitant to give even the above as it sounds like bragging. However, that is not the intention. I only mention the above to show you the limited, but still significant impact an individual can have even today.

What Young India Wants

While this book covers a wide range of topics, there are

some guidelines or common themes I follow. I either comment on the system or on society. The system changes with better policies. Society changes with better values. I have a bias towards youth-based issues, as most of India is young. Corruption, education, secularism are the topics I focus on the most. And even though some people may find it preposterous, I often propose solutions in my writings. That is because if I offer no solutions, then all I am doing is ranting. We must always suggest a way out, however simplistic it may be. It is a more positive attitude towards life.

I believe India has major problems. However, I also believe they can be fixed.

Thank you for reading this long letter!

Chetan Bhagat

04 July 2012

OUR SOCIETY

For any lasting change to happen in the country, society has to change in terms of its behaviour, attitudes and values. It is easy, even fun, to blame politicians for every wrong in the nation. However, politicians only reflect what society thinks. Thus, a big focus area for me has been my commentary on Indian society. This isn't easy, as I am asking my readers to themselves take responsibility for some of the problems. However, it is necessary.

In 'Adding Values to Life', I introduce the concept and need for the common Indian values that we lack. In 'Being Rich, Being Good', I compare Western society with ours, and see if they are really as bad as we think them to be. In 'The Great Indian Social Network', I talk about the way our industry is organized—around nepotism and connections. In 'Don't Worry, Be Happy', I try to inspire Indian women. I hope you will get a better understanding of Indian society after you read this section.

Adding Values to Life

> 'What should an average Indian live,
> work and strive for in her or his life?'

People always talk about how we should respect and uphold Indian culture and abide by Indian values. So what is culture, exactly? Our culture isn't just our food, arts and traditions. In a broader sense, culture defines us—who we are as people, how we aim to live our lives, what sort of behaviour is acceptable or unacceptable and who should be rewarded or punished according to societal norms. Most important, our culture contains the implicit rules by which we live—our values. Just as an example, one might say the United States values wealth, competition, individualism and religion. These pretty much constitute the essence of American society and culture.

When we think of Indian values, we normally think of personal values such as family, religion and respect for elders. However, ask someone to articulate Indian community values and there won't be a clear answer. Do we value wealth or education? Do we value democracy, where people have a greater say in how they are governed, or do we believe in power in the hands of a select few to whom the laws don't apply? Do we value honesty or do we value getting the job done anyhow? Do we believe in frugality or do we want to show off our wealth? Do we value our local communities or do we value being part of India?

These questions have no easy answers. And there are conflicting responses to any of these in the India we see around us today. Scholars, unable to account for this conflict, make profound statements such as 'there are many Indias within India'. Some romantic types even call this 'the beauty of India, where everything is unpredictable'.

I call it confusion. Values cannot be unpredictable; they are consistent, even in volatile times. Indian society has spent a long time living with a muddled set of values. And what we are hoping for is a 'values clarification', especially for the new generation. A clear set of values helps tell people what the purpose of their lives is and what is worth working for. Values tell people what is good and important. They bind society. Social scientists believe that without values, a society could disintegrate, a risk often present in India. Religious heads believe that without values, human life is meaningless and all worldly pleasures will not lead to any satisfaction. Yes, a lack of a set of good values is why scams happen, nepotism exists and why the government doesn't care about its people. Core values are vital to any society and human being.

So why are we in such a confused state? Where have we gone wrong? Are Indians less moral, despite being the most religious people in the world? No, we are perfectly fine. Belonging to the land where Buddha and Gandhi became icons, purely on the strength of their values, means ours is a society that understands goodness. The reason there is no concrete set of Indian values yet is because the concept of India itself is new.

Just over six decades ago, there was no India. We had a collection of princely states, with kings and queens, which the British ruled at gunpoint. When the latter left, we loosely stitched these states together, cut off a large chunk with Partition and labelled the result India. After that, another revised set of values was never fully agreed upon. In sixty-five years, India has mixed, modernized and defined itself somewhat, but there is still a long way to go. Today, different subsets of society have their own set of values, which frankly doesn't help much at the national level and leads to what we have now: confusion.

It is critical that along with our efforts to build up our economy, alleviate poverty and so on, we spend time building our values. Leaders, opinion-makers and all of us in our discussions should continue to bring up this single question: what should an average Indian live, work and strive for in his life?

At present, there is no easy answer. There is also deep cynicism. But if we keep looking and contribute to the quest for the right answer, we will find it. The answer to this fundamental question will determine our Constitution, our laws and where we will go as a society and nation in times to come.

Being Rich, Being Good

> 'Haven't we always been the good guys?
> When did that change?'

On 26 October 2011, Rajat Gupta, ex-CEO of McKinsey and one of the most high-profile corporate figures in America, was arrested on insider-trading charges. He was accused of having tipped off Raj Rajaratnam, who once ran a hedge fund worth $7 billion. Rajaratnam, who, at his peak, had a net worth of $1.8 billion, has been sentenced to eleven years in prison, along with thirteen others. This would seem surprising to many who see America as a nation associated with relentless greed, materialism and consumerism.

When we were growing up, we were often told that 'Western values' are extremely harmful for society. We Indians were supposed to be more humane, loving, caring, spiritual and genuine. The West was an embodiment of all things wrong—from excess consumption to decline in family values. We were the good ones (or is it G1s these days?)

Yet, it is America that comes down hard on those who break other people's trust. Punishment for taking more than your fair share—whether through insider trading or corruption—is severe. In Gupta's case, he may not even have benefited directly—he may have merely tipped off his friend, as alleged, unaware of how that tip would be used. But still, if proven, that was reason enough for the American system to punish him.

Yes, America is materialistic. It is even greedy to a certain extent. However, Americans have created a system in which wealth is created with hard work, innovation, talent and enterprise. People who display these qualities move up in life. Every generation in America has produced several innovators and billion-dollar global corporations, created without government connections. Americans may have a hundred flaws, but they are extremely protective of their system. Anyone who tries to break it to come up in life using unfair means is punished severely. Schools and colleges have a strict honour code against cheating. And no matter how high profile the person, society doesn't flinch at teaching the wrongdoer a lesson.

We, on the other hand, don't even have good laws to prosecute the blatantly corrupt, forget insider trading. Many may not even see insider trading as wrong—we see it as a privilege of being in a position of status or power. Any Dalal Street veteran will tell you that despite regulator

SEBI's commendable efforts, insider trading is rampant among the high and mighty. This corruption is not limited to the stock market. The real-estate developer who finds out the zoning master plan of the government beforehand and pre-emptively buys real estate, is also guilty of insider trading. However, such people are never punished.

In fact, our government attacks almost every anti-corruption crusader. It is as if the governments in power resolve to protect the corrupt. Prime ministers, regardless of the scams that happen on their watch, remain in power using every excuse—from 'I did not benefit' to 'I did not know anything'. Sadly, corruption is so widespread that opposition parties have as many corrupt members as ruling parties. Hence, today, even if we want, we can't vote in an honest government.

What happened? Weren't we supposed to be the good ones? And yet, it is the greedy, Western 'baddies' who seem to be doing a better job at being just, truthful and equal. They are not only richer; they seem better, too. It is disheartening to face this ugly truth. After all, the poor person is supposed to be the better person—at least that's what they show in the movies.

Well, we don't have good leaders because in the past, we haven't cared. We've only wanted leaders from our caste or religion. We have been enamoured less by honesty, more by dynasty. We do not have a merit-based system that generates wealth, nor anything in place to protect it. The Westerners do. Hence they are richer and, in many cases, better than us. The system we have, in which there are a few kings and lots of common people, cannot generate wealth. It kills innovation and keeps the powerful as rent-seeking controllers of resources. It will eventually turn us into a nation of clerks for the world. Innovators will rule the world; we will be left to serve them. We may not get colonized politically, but we will, economically.

Can we change this? Of course we can. Society does change, even if slowly. There was a time when we used to practise sati. We realized it was wrong and now we don't practise it any more. To change, first, let us accept our shortcomings. We Indians lack some essential good values. Being part of a corrupt society has made us all somewhat corrupt. From copying assignments to faking our children's ages on railway tickets—we have all done some wrong or accepted something wrong as part of life. We need to define a set of new values and propagate them in our social circles. We also need to support positive initiatives like the Lokpal Bill. We need to remind ourselves that individuals don't matter; it is the cause that makes sense and needs support. The new Indian quest has begun. It is to be rich, and also to be good.

The Meaning of True Wealth

> 'We must teach ourselves to earn Lakshmi, not just money.'

During Diwali, we worship Lakshmi, the goddess of wealth, but although we use the word 'Lakshmi' almost as a synonym for money, they are not the same. Here, I am reminded about a panel discussion I once participated in, conducted by Oliver Stone, the director of *Wall Street* (1984). In the film, Michael Douglas played Gordon Gekko, a crafty, unscrupulous, yet dashing financier. Gekko, with his signature line 'Greed, for lack of a better word, is good', became one of the most memorable characters in US cinematic history.

I asked Oliver why he thought Gekko became so popular. He said it was because Gekko is successful, especially in terms of money. It doesn't matter that he is unethical, selfish, greedy or a terrible human being. Americans had become obsessed with material wealth in the 1980s. 'Greed is good' was just the validation they needed at the time. No one cared about a person's values; they cared about a person's money.

'Greed is good' is valid for us too. Why else do our political leaders loot the very people who elected them? Why do they stuff their own pockets with hundreds of crores, money they can't possibly spend in their lifetimes? Why would an army general want to pocket a flat meant for a soldier's widow? Why do so many intelligent, educated, respected bureaucrats succumb to corruption?

The answer is simple: money, or rather, the importance our society has begun to attach to money.

Don't get me wrong. Money is extremely important. Poverty is a disease, and surviving well in the modern world does require a certain amount of material wealth. However, above this level, people don't seek money to satisfy material needs. Beyond that level, money has other uses. There are many reasons why our politicians and government officials steal it.

One, money provides stature—bigger houses, more lavish parties and more high-end places to shop at—and gives one a certain place in society today that is 'above others'. We have newspapers filled with ads for luxury goods, as if acquiring them should be life's ultimate aim. We celebrate 'the-most-rich-and-famous' lists and idolize those who live in expensive houses. We make and avidly watch TV shows about expensive weddings and judge people by their residential addresses. Today, a woman decked in jewellery, with a designer bag and shoes, may be seen as being of a higher stature than, say, a schoolteacher in a cotton sari who teaches hundreds of kids. Executives who earn high salaries make more news than, say, brave journalists who expose scams or selfless doctors who help the poor. In such a societal setup, the temptation to seek wealth, irrespective of the means, is especially high.

Two, money gives a sense of security. This is a genuine benefit of money, as retirement planning is about building assets in your working life which can be used later. However, politicians have a greater sense of insecurity owing to the innately uncertain nature of their jobs. They can be elected to and out of office. Money stolen by politicians is often kept for their party campaigns, to fight the next election. Being in power and retaining that position is more important—and gets you more attention—than being a real leader and role model. So you have elected MPs robbing citizens. Since the majority of Indian citizens doesn't care about corruption issues and will vote based on caste, religion or even dynasty over performance, the looting never stops.

Stature and security are constructs of the mind. The irony is, no matter how much money you have, if you don't fundamentally value yourself from within, you will never realize that truth despite the crores stashed away. That is why the corrupt keep on accumulating money until they get caught. They hope the money will give them a better place in life. However, since they have stolen, not earned, the wealth, the crime gnaws at them from within and they can never be at peace. They have accumulated money for sure, but they haven't accumulated Lakshmi.

Lakshmi is wealth accumulated through honest and fair means. Money can be stolen as well, but Lakshmi brings peace and happiness to the person who earns it. Stolen money only brings emptiness to the soul. If you notice Lakshmi's idol, she has gold coins around her, signifying wealth. However, she is also seated on a lotus flower, and holds lotuses in her hands. The lotus is a symbol of purity and peace, signifying spiritual well being; a symbol of purity and beauty even in the muddy waters of the world. Without this peace, wealth has no meaning.

So, next Diwali, when you pray, ask not for money but for Lakshmi—wealth attained through pure means that keeps the mind as peaceful and beautiful as the lotus. The corrupt who steal from us don't know this difference and merely collect money. No matter how big their Diwali parties or how lavish their puja ceremonies, true Lakshmi will never come to them. She only comes to those who are pure at heart.

The Great Indian Social Network

> 'What is cooler than a million rich Indians? A billion rich Indians!'

Mark Zuckerberg is a global business icon who has penetrated the consciousness of many youngsters. The movie based on his life, *The Social Network*, helped the process. *The Social Network* tells a semi-fictional story about the creation of Facebook (based on the book *The Accidental Billionaires*). While the film is extraordinarily well made, the story it tells is even more amazing. Mark Zuckerberg, the founder of Facebook, is, at twenty-six, the youngest billionaire in the world. Mark started Facebook from his college dorm in 2004. When the company went public in 2012, its IPO was valued in billions. The movie is path-breaking in that it is about talent, talented people and a country that celebrates talent.

For only in the USA can a boy in his twenties, coming

from nowhere, create a company worth billions in eight years and the country will celebrate him by making a movie on him. Ironically, Mark never cared about making money when he founded Facebook. His main motivation was to do something innovative, entrepreneurial and, most importantly, cool. At one point in the film, he states, 'Money, or the ability to make money, doesn't impress anyone around here.'

Compare this to India's celebrated businessmen. The corporate czars we celebrate—with some exceptions— are second- or third-generation tycoons who run huge empires comprising dozens of unrelated businesses. Traditional management theory will wonder how a company can be in food, telecom, power, construction and financial sectors all at the same time. However, in India, such conglomerates thrive. The promoters of these companies have the required skill—navigating the Indian government maze. Whether it is obtaining permission to set up a power plant, or to use agricultural land for commercial purposes, or to obtain licences to open a bank or sell liquor—our top business promoters can get all this done, something ordinary Indians would never be able to. This is why they are able to make billions. We then load them with awards, rank them on lists and treat them as role models for the young.

In reality, they are hardly icons. They have milked an unfair system for their personal benefit, taking opportunities that would have belonged to the young on a level playing field. Indian companies make money from rent-seeking behaviour, creating artificial barriers of access to regulators, thereby depriving our start-ups of wealth-generating opportunities. None of the recent technologies that have changed the world and created wealth—telecom, computers, aviation—have come out of India. Yet, our promoters have figured out a way to make money from them by bulldozing their way into their share of the pie, rationing out the technology to Indians and setting themselves up as modern-day heroes. In reality, they are no heroes. They are the opposite of cool and, despite their billions, they are what young people call 'losers'.

For if they are not losers, why have they never raised their voices against governmental corruption? Our corporate honchos don't think twice before creating a cartel to fleece customers. Yet they have never even thought about creating a cartel to take a stand against corrupt politicians. They scream about the Radia tapes being leaked but do not reflect on their disgusting content. None of our blue chips have the capability to invent technology like the cell phone but being opportunists, they jump at the chance of making money off spectrum allocation.

International investors already know this, and while they see India's potential, they understand that the Indian corporate–political nexus is actually keeping the country poor, not making it rich.

This can be fixed. Quite frankly, it *has* to be fixed if we want India to be the great nation our forefathers dreamed of. The net effect of this nepotism is high—it's often debilitating for start-ups in India, vital to the broad-based growth of any economy. If we want to set this right, there is a role to be played by corporate houses, the government and individuals.

First, the few corporations who really care have to form a cartel against corruption and nepotism. If promoters take a public stand that their business group will not pay bribes, it will send a strong message. They should compete on innovation, not the ability to bribe. That's what is cool. Meanwhile, the current billionaires should stop flaunting their money and consider the fifty-seven richest billionaires of America who pledged to give away more than half their wealth to charity (yes, Mark Zuckerberg included).

Second, our government has to understand the meaning of protecting Indian industry. It isn't to protect the established fat cats, who could, frankly, do with a dose of healthy competition. Protecting Indian industry means evolving policies that help new Indian companies thrive, an environment where start-ups are glorified and inherited princes are not put on a pedestal. Innovation, not inheritance, should be considered cool.

Third, we, as individuals, have to stop admiring and glorifying the parasitic billionaires of India. They may not be doing anything illegal technically, but there is definitely nothing great about using connections to get something you couldn't have had if there was fair competition. We should be celebrating innovation and entrepreneurship, not money, consumption and power.

Yes, these businessmen employ some of us, and we have seen increased affluence amongst some of our fellows. Maybe we have a million rich Indians now. But it isn't enough. With the right business environment, India can be a dramatically different place, offering a better life to not just a few, but to all of us. After all, to modify a dialogue from the film, 'You know what's cooler than a million rich Indians? A billion rich Indians.'

The Great Indian Psychotherapy

> 'We resolve to vote on the basis
> of performance alone, nothing else.'

Countless articles, books, theses, papers and research reports have tried to answer the question: 'What is wrong with India?' Global experts are startled that a country of such massive potential has one of the largest percentages of poor people in the world. Isn't it baffling that despite almost everyone agreeing that things should change, they don't? Intellectuals give their intelligent suggestions—from investing in infrastructure to improving the judicial system. Yet, nothing moves. Issues dating back to thirty years continue to plague India today. The young are often perplexed by this. They ask, will things ever change? How? Whose fault is it that they haven't?

Today, I will attempt to answer these tricky questions, although from a different perspective. I will not put the blame on everyone's favourite punching bags—inept politicians. That is too easy an argument and not entirely correct. After all, *we* elect the politicians. So, for every MP out there, there are a few lakh people who chose him or her. I won't give 'policy' solutions either—build power plants, improve roads, open up the economy. It isn't the lack of such ideas that is stalling progress. No, blocking progress is part of Indians' unique psyche. There are three traits of our psyche, in particular, that are not good for our country and for us. Each comes from three distinct sources—our school, our environment and our home.

The first trait is servility. At school, our education system hammers out our individual voices and kills our natural creativity, turning us into servile, course-material slaves. Our kids are not encouraged to raise their voices in class, particularly when they disagree with the teacher. And of course, no subject teaches us imagination, creativity or innovation. Curricula are designed for the no debate kind of teaching. For example, we ask: how many states are there in India? Answer: Twenty-eight. Correct. Next question: how is a country divided into states? What criteria should be used? No answer. Since issues like these are never discussed, children never develop their own viewpoint or the faculty to think.

The second trait is our numbness to injustice. It comes from our environment. We are exposed to corruption from our childhood. Almost all of us have been asked to lie about our ages to the train ticket-checker, to claim to be less than five years old and get a free train ride. This creates a value system in a child's brain that 'anything goes' so long as you can get away with it. A bit of lying here, a bit of cheating there is seen as acceptable. Hence, we all grow up slightly numb to corruption.

The third trait is divisiveness. This is often taught at our home, particularly our family and relatives, where we learn about the differences amongst people. Our religion, culture and language are revered and celebrated in our families. Other people are different—and often implied to be not as good as us. We've all known an aunt or uncle who, though a good person, holds rigid biases against people from different communities. Even today, most of India votes on one criterion—caste. Dalits vote for dalits, Thakurs for Thakurs and Yadavs for Yadavs. In such a scenario, why would a politician do any real work? When we choose a mobile network, do we check whether Airtel or Vodafone belong to a particular caste? No, we simply choose the provider based on the best value or service. Then why do we vote for somebody simply because he belongs to the same caste as us?

We need mass self-psychotherapy for the three traits listed above. When we talk of change, you and I alone can't get a politician replaced, or order a road to be built. However, we can change one thing—our mindset. And collectively, this has the power to make the biggest difference. We have to unlearn whatever is holding us back and definitely break the cycle so that we don't pass on these traits to the next generation. Our children should think creatively, have opinions and speak up. They should learn that what is wrong is wrong, no matter how big or small. And they shouldn't hate other people on the basis of their background. Let us also resolve to start working on our own minds, right now. A change in mindset changes the way people vote, which, in turn, changes politicians.

And change does happen. In the 1980s, we had movies like *Gunda* and *Khoon Pi Jaaonga*. Today, our movies have better content. They have changed. How? It is because our expectations from films have changed. Hence, the filmmakers had to change.

If we resolve today that we will vote on the basis of performance alone, we will encourage the voices against injustice. If we place an honest, though less wealthy person on a higher pedestal than a corrupt, yet rich individual, we will have contributed to India's progress. And then, maybe, we will start moving towards a better India. Are you on board?

The Wrong Diagnosis

> 'What India needs is a course of antibiotics;
> Crocin is just not working.'

More often than not, violent and disturbing images fill our television screens during news telecasts. It is no wonder. Seven Naxal-affected states, disturbances in all seven north-eastern states and, of course, the ever-present strife in Kashmir—fifteen of India's twenty-eight states have some internal conflict or the other. In addition, we also have religion/caste/regionalism-based violence in other parts of the country. If that's not enough, add honour killings to the list. While no one strife dominates, we are probably living in one of the most violent times in independent India. All this, at a time when India is touted to be one of the fastest growing economies in the world, when we have a relatively stable government and we see more affluence around us than at any other time. Three questions come to mind: what's going on? Where will all this lead? Most importantly, what can be done about it?

The answer to the first question—what's going on?—can be the same cynical response: this is what India is. Blame the politicians, corrupt officials, illiterate voters and that seems to work. The question can also be answered by the usual 'who cares', especially for us city dwellers who don't really see the impact of these fifteen-odd conflicts. The Naxalites haven't attacked our five-star hotels, cinemas and train stations—yet—and the north-east movements are too far away to be noticed. However, we have to care. Because the next question—where will all this lead to?—is simply not being discussed enough.

The fact is that despite liberalization of the economy, benefits are not reaching everyone. Yes, they reach the top 10 per cent. However, the other 90 per cent are still untouched. In fact, these people get the worst of badly implemented capitalism —inflation kills their savings and purchasing power, their land gets stolen by corporate houses and their politician cares only about the rich guys. They are not in any advertiser's target group so the media dismisses them and they don't get a voice. Every now and then, a politician tosses cheap rice or wheat at them, keeps them alive on drip feed, and hopes to swing some votes. Our rural poor never see the benefits of liberalization. Add to this, poor education, archaic caste-based social discrimination, poorly implemented welfare policies and a general lack of job opportunities, and it leads to a kind of passive frustration that urban citizens can never understand. The leaders of these movements apparently do, and that is why a youth, with his whole life ahead of him, takes up arms against the state and becomes a rebel.

So while we might debate endlessly on whether the CRPF is adequate to fight the Naxals, or whether the army is doing a good job in Kashmir, the fact is that in these discussions, we are only addressing the symptoms. We are trying to bring the fever down when the infection is what needs to be cured. We don't need Crocin; we need strong antibiotics. And unless the rural or underprivileged Indian youth sees a better life coming, the infection is only going to grow. From fifteen states, the infection could spread to all twenty-eight states. Trouble is brewing, and the cities are ignoring it.

The final question—what can be done about it?—is what we need to spend most of our time on. For one, better politicians, who are committed to developing their local areas, need to be elected. However, currently, they can't be. In the interiors, as I have mentioned earlier, the single-most important criterion for voting is caste. No matter how capable a candidate, if you don't match the voter's caste, you will not get his vote. In such a scenario, there is no incentive for a candidate to do a good job. Managing his caste alliances is the only real job he has. And since most of our candidates come from the interiors, we end up with a bunch of politicians who have given us the India we have today. How will this change? The urban–rural connection needs to be made significantly stronger. Our most educated and forward-thinking citizens are in the cities. While still a small proportion of the total population, these educated people can be ambassadors for a new India in the villages.

One suggestion is to use the massive student population. A radical move—such as exchange programmes between urban and rural colleges—where every city student spends time in the villages, and vice versa, will help a lot. This needs to be done on a massive scale. The city students will spend time in the villages, infuse modern values there, and come back with a better understanding of rural issues. There can be other similar ideas, such as incentivizing MNCs to base themselves in smaller towns. Sure, there will be lots of challenges but, frankly, there is no other way out. Unless we truly reform the core of our country, things will never really change.

One insurgency curtailed will turn into another, TV anchors will scream, politicians will offer a Crocin and the infection will continue to spread. Surely that's not the India we want to leave behind for the next generation. It's time to pop the antibiotics and, most importantly, complete the course.

Mandi Economics

'Today, it is the farmer who needs nourishment.'

On my way to another city, I was at the airport to board a flight. I was told that the flight was delayed. I was disappointed but had no choice. As compensation, the airline gave me one sandwich. After three hours, they told me the flight had been cancelled. However, this time they gave me two sandwiches. I argued about my missed flight. How would I reach my destination? They said they were a caring airline and so they could give me three sandwiches. The flight never took off. What would you want to do with such an airline? Would you call it a caring people's carrier?

No, I am not talking about any particular airline or ranting about my mishap at the airport. I'm merely creating an analogy for the attitude of the government towards farmers. On the surface, they are provided subsidies, loan waivers and cheap rice. However, none of these measures create real progress or change the face of agriculture in India.

And before we start blaming the rain gods yet again, I want to know why we are so dependent on rain-fed agriculture even now. If India is an agricultural country, shouldn't we have carried out some massive infrastructure projects across the country? Over two-thirds of our agricultural land is dependent on rain. In contrast, only one-third of China's land is not irrigated. Developed countries depend very little on rain, as this dependence creates high fluctuations in the output, year after year. Apart from the volatility, we are not efficient either. China can produce twice the amount of rice for every acre of land than us. Australia can produce five times the rice per acre than India.

Let's face it, the Indian farmer is not cared for. He is on drip feed in a hospital, sustained by subsidies and being kept alive only for votes. The cheap rice one-upmanship seems great in the short term, but will it help close the massive efficiency gap or the rain dependence? And if this gap is not closed, can India ever really progress? There are other downsides of subsidies too. The government has to borrow increasing amounts of money, which, in turn, leads to higher capital costs for power and transportation infrastructure projects. It also leads to inflation.

Yes, we can continue to live like this: constantly rising prices; the rare infrastructure project that is too little too late; and poverty, with its attendant problems of poor healthcare and low literacy. But we have yet another option:

all this can change. Many south-east Asian countries were in a similar situation twenty years ago. However, these countries have implemented sound economic policies, focused on massive long-term developmental projects (rather than cheap vote-bank politics) and changed the face of their countryside.

While it is easy to blame politicians, it is also true that we elect them. And the fact is that subsidies do result in votes. The intoxication of cheap rice is heady. It makes the voter believe that the government is doing something. A lot of people may even think, Grab whatever you can. The government won't do anything else anyway. But can we sustain this? Is this good for the country in the long term? Do you want to give your children the same India that you inherited or do you want to leave them with a better, improved country?

Development in agriculture is not only about setting up irrigation projects and enhancing crop yields. There are many other areas of improvement. In Hong Kong and Singapore, milk and butter are imported all the way from Australia. If an Indian software company can provide service abroad, there is no reason why an Indian farmer should be denied such a lucrative market.

However, there are some who argue that we need to keep the milk for our own country. There are two holes in that argument. One, if a farmer makes more money, he will invest in more cattle or in improving the efficiency of his farm, thus helping production levels rise to meet demand in India as well as abroad. Two, we (rightly) don't force our corporate sector companies to sell their products exclusively in India. Then how can we force the farmer? To cut off a source of income and then offer cheap rice—is that caring for our rural citizens?

The government and quasi-government entities keep a tight control on dairy and farm produce for food-security reasons. However, the fear is overblown and excessive Government involvement has prevented world-class output. Food that isn't grown due to poor efficiency is food destroyed. The government is not saving food, it is destroying it. There are several companies who operate worldwide. While they are private enterprises, they have benefited millions around the world. Let's demand the same world-class treatment from our leaders.

Agriculture can be India's competitive strength globally if we become serious about it. The Indian farmer feeds us. We must nourish the nourisher to ensure he will still be around, for us and for generations to come.

Shopping for Consensus

> 'Setting off a bomb in class is a temporary solution; we need to do our homework.'

The debate about allowing foreign direct investment (FDI) in the retail sector brought back a school memory. Once, in class VII, a strict teacher gave us a challenging assignment as homework. On the due date, most students had not done it. However, just prior to the teacher's arrival, someone had a brainwave. He planted a Diwali bomb with a long fuse under a vacant desk. The teacher arrived. Within a minute, a deafening noise interrupted class.

Shocked, the teacher rushed out and brought back the headmistress. Throughout the rest of the period, both of them tried to figure out who set off the bomb and gave us lectures on our rowdy behaviour. The culprits were never found. The period ended in an hour. We breathed a sigh of relief. Nobody had cared about the homework.

This is rather like the needless uproar over the government's proposal to introduce FDI in retail—a meaningless distraction at best, a real disservice to the nation at worst. Reason suggests we cannot afford to turn up our noses at FDI. The aspirations of India's massive population cannot be met by the capital generated internally. We have opened up many sectors to FDI. In all these sectors, service quality has improved while the domestic industry has survived. Yes, the FDI investor makes a return, but not as a handout. The investor does the work and takes the risk.

Our banks have thrived even after foreign banks came into the country. Telecom, insurance, software—there are innumerable examples of FDI working well in India. Where it hasn't worked well is usually because we created regulations that never actually opened up the sector for business.

Even in FDI in retail, a more sensitive issue, it is unlikely that it will kill our domestic small-scale retail. Indian mega corporations have already entered the retail sector, but the neighbourhood kirana stores and the street vendors still survive quite well. These new Indian chains have provided a superior shopping experience. They have also created jobs and treat their employees better than the kirana store-owners who have no employee welfare policies to speak of. The Philippines, Thailand, Malaysia and China—all of these countries have allowed foreign retail stores and there has been no significant impact on the local industry.

Hence, FDI in retail is one of the rare issues on which one can actually agree with the UPA government. But it must be said that however well intentioned the initiative may have been, the way the UPA handled it was a bit of a disaster.

If the entire FDI-in-retail issue was planned to be the bomb in the classroom, a shrewd political move to distract from other controversial ones, it backfired. If it was done without thinking, then, of course, that made it so much worse. What it exposed was the Congress's inability and unwillingness to build consensus on almost anything. Forget opposition parties and allies, even Congress members did not like the way the policy was thrust on them. The power of the family brand is useful to keep dissent under wraps but some chinks do show through. After all, it must be suffocating to be in the Congress for some capable leaders who are completely ignored, simply because they are not close enough to the family. This internal simmering within the Congress is a bigger threat to it than the opposition.

The FDI retail drama exposed a recurring problem with BJP as well—the party's inability to manage outrageous statements by its leaders. One of their leaders wanted to burn Walmart stores down. Great going, madam. Tens of thousands of our software programmers work in the US. Our call centres have taken many US jobs. Should they burn us down, too? The BJP has many good orators but no restraint.

The issue of FDI in retail is a free-for-all. However, if and when some sense prevails, the government, with humility, should involve everyone in Parliament to get a general policy consensus on FDI, not just for retail but for all sectors across all industries.

Coming back to the school story, the next day, the teacher came to class and asked for the assignment. Those who hadn't done it were punished, and extra severely, due to the Diwali bomb set off the previous day. Distraction works, but only for a while. Ultimately, the homework has to be done.

Altitude Sickness

'How did no one notice when the Kingfisher lost its wings?'

I was on board a Delhi–Bangalore Kingfisher flight. As I was typing, a lovely lady served me a tomato mozzarella sandwich on a beautiful white plate and her smile as she did so made it impossible to guess that the airline she worked for was in trouble. However, the truth of the matter was that the airline had received enormous negative coverage in the media, Kingfisher had racked up enormous losses and owed its creditors several thousand crore rupees.

These are mind-boggling numbers. Surely this level of debt and losses were not accumulated overnight. How did Kingfisher reach this point where several of its jets were grounded, caterers refused to supply sandwiches and airports wouldn't let flights take off until the airline paid in cash? Didn't the stakeholders involved—lenders, directors, vendors and others—ever express concern? What kept it going? Financial analysts across the world will agree that the airline sector is one of the worst sectors to make money from and offers the poorest returns. The business requires huge capital investments upfront, competition is intense and customers are price sensitive. These factors affect the Indian airline sector even more because here, interest rates are high, customers are extraordinarily price sensitive and the government regulations and taxes are crippling. And yet, there are plenty of entrepreneurs who want to have their own airline. Wonder why?

Well, let's face it, there are few businesses as sexy as owning an airline. You could be making hundreds of crores as a fertilizer manufacturer, a packaging plant owner or a garment exporter. Yet, at one level, all these businesses are boring. Who cares if you have a thirty-acre, money-spinning industrial plant in a remote town? However, if you have a dozen planes—flying on borrowed money, of course—you are the new man in town. Good-looking pilots, charming flight attendants, flight schedules, exhilarating takeoffs, all make the 30,000-feet-in-the-sky business oh so sexy. It is almost as glamorous as Bollywood.

Due to this sexiness, everyone wants to be a part of it. Public sector banks line up to lend an airline thousands of crores. This for a mere couple of points more interest than if they had invested in risk-free but oh-so-dull RBI bonds. Netas—even our super-elusive prime minister felt, at one point in time, the need to make a comment about helping Kingfisher—and babus love to get involved in the airlines business. Incidentally, that is the main reason why another money-burner, Air India, is still alive.

The airline industry is seen as a glamour industry, when, in reality, it is anything but that. It is a dull, horrible, never-ending quest to cut costs, meet demanding schedules and keep the planes busy. It is not much different from a logistics, courier or any other transportation company. Most of the profitable airlines in the world are cost-cutters. Some have scraped off paint from the planes to reduce extra weight. Others have shaved inches of legroom to add an extra row.

The winners have the lowest cost and are thus able to offer the lowest prices which fill the maximum number of seats. Indigo does this in India, and is still profitable despite the draconian tax structures (which definitely need revision). A few luxury airlines do exist, but they serve extraordinarily affluent markets with a high number of senior business travellers. They also serve cities that are global business hubs—for instance, SIA in Singapore, Cathay Pacific in Hong Kong and Emirates in Dubai. Even these airlines run a very efficient economy class.

Kingfisher's business model, in hindsight, was flawed from the start. A focus on flamboyance and opulence in a super-price-sensitive industry was extremely unlikely to work. And it never did in financial terms. Banks could have spotted this years ago and pulled the plug on the company, leading to a far more manageable situation. However, who cares about a few thousand crores of depositors' money when the party is so much fun?

The Kingfisher management's claim that the government tax structure led to the decline was only partially correct. And while the tax structure for airlines does need reform, it is also true that all airlines have to pay the same onerous taxes. It was Kingfisher's fundamental business model that had a problem and all stakeholders involved needed to face up to it.

Despite what the parties involved and the government say, it is not easy to fix Kingfisher. The debt levels and current losses are too high to engineer a quick turnaround. Someone has to take the pain, and most likely, it will be the banks that were stupid enough to lend so much money in the first place— and might just lend some more. To make matters worse, some of these banks are public sector banks so, indirectly, we people will pay for the extravagance and the bad business judgments of a few.

After my sandwich, the flight attendant arrived with dessert and I could not resist asking if she knew about the airline's problems. She said she didn't know much, but her salary had been delayed and some people were scaring her about the airline's future. When asked what she thought would happen, she said, 'This is just like turbulence. Sit tight with your seatbelts on, and it will pass.' One can only hope so.

What's a Citizen's Life Worth?

> 'The common man's life should be more valuable than a company's profit, shouldn't it?'

Imagine, you kiss your child good night. You go back to your room to sleep. During the night, poisonous gases fill your child's room, suffocating him. The gases enter your room, killing you too. I am sorry to create this gory visual, and hope and pray this never happens to you. However, this is precisely what happened to thousands of families in Bhopal in 1984.

Many factors led to—and could have prevented—the incident. The location of a poisonous pesticide factory so close to the city, poor maintenance of equipment, cutting corners on safety by management, previous warnings about plant safety, labour issues—all these have been identified by studies, post the incident. There are clearly two guilty parties—the company, Union Carbide, that owned the plant and various government authorities that gave approvals for it.

More disturbing was the post-incident handling of affairs by the government. It is reported that the government actually assisted Warren Anderson, CEO of Union Carbide India Limited, in leaving the country. The seven other accused were punished after twenty-five years, getting a maximum of two years' sentences, and were out on bail after paying bond of Rs 25,000 each.

Compare this to the oil spill in the Gulf of Mexico, in 2010, sixty-five kilometres away from the US shoreline. The spill started in April due to an explosion on board Deepwater Horizon, an offshore drilling rig leased by BP, one of the world's leading oil exploration companies. Eleven people died in the explosion and seventeen people were injured. The spill also caused significant damage to marine life and ecology.

The US government spared no effort in bringing BP to book. Hundreds of lawsuits were filed against BP. Barack Obama himself made several anger-filled statements about BP's 'recklessness' and 'doing what it takes' to get BP to fix it. Such was the fear of the US government's resolve to teach the company a lesson that its shares lost close to $105 billion since the spill. BP also created a $20 billion trust to compensate claims and paid about $8 billion in damages. (Incidentally, the Bhopal accused were let out on bail for a fraction of that that amount.) BP, on the other hand, had to cut its dividends and has spent billions trying to plug the leak.

That's how you teach big corporations a lesson. You make the cost of playing with safety so high that they never even dream of shortcuts. While it is unfortunate that one incident can wipe out a global corporate, there is no other choice. One big guy punished changes the way thousands of other companies think. I can bet that every oil company thoroughly evaluated its safety procedures after the BP incident. To protect marine life and related industries, even the business-friendly US government was ready to—as a White House spokesman said—'put the boot on BP's neck'.

Back home, it is a different story. In several villages in Punjab, kids have developed neurological problems and deformities as there is uranium in the water due to pollution by nearby plants. And Bhopal, the mother of all industrial disasters, serves as an example of how little our government values Indian citizens' lives.

Let there be no doubt, the government is as much a culprit in Bhopal as Union Carbide. Every plant approval, safety norm and inspection also involves government authorities. Palms are greased, relationships are made and the good Indian businessmen learn to manage government officials. After all, the skill of doing business in India lies in managing the system, not innovation or better products. The nexus between the rich and government servants is strong and you will often find one in the other's living room in the evenings.

Why do so many politicians socialize with industrialists? They bond over dinners and plan their kids' education and their wives' shopping trips. At parties, they shake hands over approvals. It all seems perfectly harmless. What's wrong with making friends? However, trouble happens when disaster strikes. The first person the politician/bureaucrat helps is the industrialist, not the suffering people. I'm sure Anderson knew the right people. And he used his contacts to make his escape. The little kid who got gassed didn't have contacts. Neither did he have a government representative who would bang his fists on the table to get him justice. Because, quite simply, people in India are cheaper than fish.

All hope is not lost, however. We can still learn our lessons and do a couple of things right. One, our laws need to be amended for corporate disasters. Corporates make a mistake, they have to pay—heavily. Two, politician-industrialist socializing should not be encouraged. While a politician making social visits to industrialists can't be banned, it should definitely be disclosed. Only then will, perhaps, an ordinary citizen's life be valued higher than a company's profit.

Chocolate Cake and Terror

> 'We'd rather eat chocolate cake than waste time hating another community or country.'

In 2009, when I last visited the German Bakery in Pune, my twin sons insisted on having a slice of chocolate cake. I told them we could have it next time, since we drove down to the city so often on weekends anyway. But I was unable to keep my promise, for the next image I saw was of the bakery blown to bits. A newspaper sketch showed that the bomb was placed exactly where my family used to sit: in the outdoor area. My first thought after the attack was, it could have been us.

German Bakery was not a particularly upscale place—dishes there cost far less than at other coffee-shop chains. It had a relaxed vibe, due to the monk-robed Osho ashram customers. Ironically, it was one of the last places you would associate with violence. Almost every college student or young professional in Pune would have visited this popular youth hangout. It was not surprising that many of the dead were young students.

The first reaction to such a horrific incident is emotional. The more you relate to the event, the more difficult it becomes to think straight. Feelings of rage, despair and grief intermingle. Media reports, whether intentionally or not, repeatedly play up the horror, tap into this emotion and increase it.

'Is anyone safe?' 'Was the police sleeping?' 'It's the politicians' fault' 'Screw all talk of peace, bomb Pakistan' are phrases tossed around on TV, the Internet and in conversations. I understand the mental state where such comments come from. However, such outcries do not help solve the problem. In fact, stew such emotions too long and the mood becomes ripe for a politician to sway people into hating a particular country and a particular religion. And at the end, the root problem is not addressed.

The problem, at a factual level, is about a few deranged people who can, relatively easily, toss a bomb or fire guns at innocent people at a popular venue and attract almost immediate attention worldwide. This attention is the biggest incentive for such an act. These people, or terrorists, also have a twisted moral justification. They do not perceive their victims to be innocent, even if the victim's 'crime', in their heads, is belonging to a particular religion or country. Also, these terrorists do not place a very high value on their own lives, for in many cases they get caught or killed.

How do you deal with such a problem? It is certainly not easy. Venue-specific security measures help for sure. However, the solution lies in addressing four areas—managing the randomness of the acts, curtailing the availability of explosives, limiting the media attention and improving opportunities to limit dissatisfaction among the populace.

The first step is to reduce the randomness. There isn't much one can do if a lunatic decides to launch a shooting spree at a random venue. However, it should be noted that there is a finite number of such maniacs. Also, it doesn't represent the character trait of a particular country or community. Even if there are 10,000 terrorists, that's still only 0.001 per cent of our population.

Also, while spread out, given the logistics required and their ideology, terrorists will be connected. Akin to social networking sites, there has to be a loose structure that puts them at least in various clusters, if not one organization. It makes any terrorist caught alive, or other leads such as phone records, extremely valuable. This mapping could make finding them less random. This effort has to be led by an independent, empowered and capable organization. The same people who solve domestic robbery cases may not have the bandwidth, though on the ground, police can sniff out leads.

Second, curtail the easy availability of explosives. Try finding RDX in China—you'll be in jail before you figure out the acronym. However, in India, a newspaper sting operation team obtained it in a couple of hours. Why can't we successfully ban RDX and all such dangerous compounds? Maybe RDX has some legitimate uses, but given how a bagful of it can shatter the nation's spirit, is it worth it? Surely explosives are manufactured somewhere, or imported across the border at some venue. Can't the people involved be hunted down?

The third step is to limit the attention, particularly the emotional aspects, given by the media to such attacks. While news has to be reported, guidelines can be drawn up between TV channels on how much gore and suffering has to be shown versus the actual facts of the event.

The fourth and final step is the long-drawn one, where a country must develop to create opportunities for young people so that there is less likelihood of people choosing to become terrorists. Anyone with a good education, a job and an optimistic view on life is less likely to blow up a peaceful place.

We cannot take away the pain felt by all affected. However, rational steps can reduce such horrific acts. They will make way for a more peaceful and better life for Indians, who'd much rather have chocolate cake with their kids than live a life hating another community or country.

Game for a Clean-up

'Cricket: India's favourite game or dirtiest?'

Many decades ago, my little brother and I used to spend our evenings in neighbourhood parks where we played only one game: cricket. We watched every Test match on TV. We idolized the players and tore up sports magazines to put our heroes' photos on our room walls. We used to scavenge used soft-drink bottle caps for months to win a silly flip book which animated a player's stroke play. We weren't alone; almost every kid in school behaved the same way. Not much has changed since. Indians are still hooked to their favourite game, which is both a passion and an addiction.

A couple of centuries ago, the British entered China with a unique strategy. They got the population hooked on opium. The British had a monopoly on the drug, which they grew in India. The Chinese couldn't have enough of it. That monopoly was enough to change the entire geopolitics of the region. This dodgy trade eventually led to several wars. Of course, cricket isn't exactly opium. Opium was actually bad for people and turned the population unproductive. Cricket doesn't have the same negative effects. However, the mechanism by which the Indian cricket business operates is not too different from the drug business of the past. Two main factors are common: a deep desire among the local population to consume the product and a de facto monopoly on the business. Not to mention the complete opaqueness on the part of the monopolizer. Not surprisingly, both the businesses ended up being about big money, power and murkiness. The same thing happened with the IPL.

The IPL was, after all, the new hit drug. A quick fix of sixes and other sexy things, without the boring bits that made up the actual game. In fact, India didn't even have to win against another country to get high on this one. Indians lapped it up, advertisers supported it and the party was on.

But then came the big money, then the powerful people and then, the murkiness. The party could have continued if they had followed the first rule of running a cartel: keep a low profile. However, just like Denzel Washington in *American Gangster*, who wore a flashy fur coat that did him in, a few brash tweets happened. What followed was the explosion called the IPL controversy, which, frankly, is far more interesting than watching those silly quickie matches, whose outcome depends more on randomness than the actual talent of players. IPL had already mixed cricket and Bollywood, now it had politics, too. What more could Indians ask for from India's biggest reality show? Too bad IPL didn't sell the controversy rights beforehand. It would have been a better source of income than the 'chat up the cheerleader' helpline (no kidding, there is such a service).

While this is interesting drama, there is no denying the pressing need to clean up the BCCI. For, even though the game is a national passion, it doesn't have to be operated like a drug cartel. The BCCI has repeatedly shied away from disclosure, citing itself as a private entity. However, it isn't completely private either, especially since it has monopoly rights over something consumed by a large number of people. It earns from franchise owners and television networks. They, in turn, recover their money from advertisers, who ultimately pass on advertising costs to consumers, built into the price of products. Thus, the consumers, we Indians, pay for the BCCI. And since it is a monopoly, we have every right to question their finances. How does the BCCI price its rights? Where is the BCCI money going?

Before the limelight shifts to another drama, the media and lawmakers have a chance to go after this completely feudal and archaic way of managing something as pure and simple as sport. Individuals are less important than changing the way things work. What needs to be at the forefront is sport; are we using the money to help develop it in the country?

We don't have to turn Indian cricket into a non-commercial NGO, for that is doomed to fail. It is fine to commercially harness the game. However, if you exploit a national passion, funded by the common man, it only makes sense that the money is accounted for and utilized for the best benefit of sport in the country.

For, if there is less opaqueness, there won't be any need to make influential calls or petty factors like personality clashes affecting the outcome of any bidding process. If we know where the money is going, there is less chance of murkiness entering the picture. Accountability does not mean excessive regulation or a lack of autonomy. It simply means proper audited accounts, disclosures, corporate governance practices, norms to regulate the monopoly and even specific data on the improvement in sporting standards achieved in the country.

If a young child grows up seeing cricket as yet another example of India's rich and powerful treating the country as their fiefdom, it won't be a good thing. Let's clean up the mess and treat cricket as it is supposed to be: a good sport.

Don't Worry, Be Happy

'Aren't we expecting too much from our women?.'

All right, this is not cool at all. A survey by Nielsen revealed that Indian women are the most stressed out in the world: 87 per cent of our women feel stressed most of the time. This statistic alone caused me to stress out. Even in workaholic America, only 53 per cent women feel stressed.

What are we doing to our women? I may be biased, but Indian women are the most beautiful in the world. As mothers, sisters, daughters, colleagues, wives and girlfriends, we love them. Can you imagine life without these ladies? It would be a universe full of messy, aggressive and egomaniacal males running the world, trying to outdo each other for no particular reason. There would be body odour, socks on the floor and nothing in the fridge to eat. The entertainment industry would die. Who wants to watch movies without actresses?

Kids would be neglected and turn into drug addicts or psychopaths by age ten. Soon, all-male world leaders would lose their tempers at the slightest provocation and bomb the guts out of each other's countries. In short, without women and their sanity, the world would perish.

Yet, look at how we Indians, a land of spiritual people, treat them. At an extreme, we abort girls before they are born, neglect their upbringing, torture them, molest them, sell them, rape them and honour-kill them. Of course, these criminal acts are performed by a tiny minority.

However, a majority of us are involved in lesser crimes. We judge our women, expect too much of them, don't give them space and suffocate their individuality. Imagine, if you did this to men—wouldn't they get stressed out?

At a broader level, this isn't just about our women. We Indians have a habit of exploiting anyone without power. As a flip side, we are suckers for anyone with power. We look up to corrupt politicians, keep voting them back and feel they are entitled to loot us silly, just because they are in power. In fact, we love power so much that when power comes to a woman, we automatically begin to regard her well, too. Goddesses, female politicians, senior mothers in a household with a firm grip on family power—they all get our respect. Anyone else doesn't.

POLITICS

If you want to change things in a democracy, you cannot stay away from politics. Political writing was, and still is, uncharted territory for me. It has been a hit-and-miss ride, and several times I have earned extreme reactions. In my defense, I can only say that I am neutral in terms of political parties, commenting always on issues rather than personalities.

In 'India's Democratic Princes', I try to explain why we still have dynasty politics. In 'Return of the Brash Politician', I talk about how new-age politicians are bolder than before. In 'Getting Realistic about Real Estate', I suggest that land is a huge asset which the government can unlock to create value. In 'How to Reverse the Trust Deficit', I try to bring both sides in the Lokpal Bill agitation, civil society and the government, together on the same page.

Indian politics is a jigsaw puzzle that can take decades to understand. I hope that this section will give you a flavour of what it is like to be part of the biggest democracy in the world.

Don't Let Them Divide and Rule Anymore

> 'Vote bank politics seems to have become our new divide-and-rule policy.'

Sometimes, I wonder what it would be like to be a member of an oppressed Indian minority community. I am neither a Muslim, nor a dalit. I am not a woman. I don't even belong to the north-east; people from there are often discriminated against in various parts of India. The closest I felt to being part of a minority was when I worked abroad in a bank and experienced the occasional tinge of discrimination against Indians. Still, that was insignificant.

In a sense, I can never fully understand the feelings a person from a minority community goes through. Hence, any attempt to give advice to members of minority communities of India is audacious. None of us who belong to majority communities are completely qualified to comment on their situation.

A better India requires better leaders, something we have to work together for. We have to learn to vote better. We haven't been doing so, and that is why we often find some of the most dishonest people in society right at the top. Perhaps we have a bad system, or we don't know how to vote. Most likely, the candidates managed to fool us.

One way some politicians fool us is by playing vote bank politics. They understand the oppression felt by the minority community, claim to be their saviours, and ask for their vote in return. The member of the minority community votes for the candidate or party in the hope that it will come to power and protect them. Unfortunately, that does not happen. What happens is that the wrong guy is chosen for the job, someone who is neither competent, nor honest. He is chosen only because he is a symbol of hope for the minority. Decades pass and the minority community remains as oppressed as ever. Of all the minorities lured into such deceptive vote bank schemes, our Muslim citizens are wooed the most because their community is one of the largest in terms of actual numbers. Also, as a community, they face significant oppression. Appeal to that injustice, and one can bring them all together and, hopefully, get a nice block vote for a politician.

My dear Muslim brothers and sisters, you have been had. Yes, you have been fooled time and again by these politicians who promised you the world, but kept you as oppressed as ever. They may have given you an odd freebie, but they kept the whole nation poor due to bad governance. They never built proper infrastructure, irrigation facilities, enough schools, colleges or healthcare facilities to make sure citizens enjoy a respectable life. Yes, they have fooled the whole nation. They kept us busy with the Hindu versus Muslim debate while they hid the fact that the entire country suffered due to their misgovernment. For when a student doesn't get into a good college, it doesn't matter if he is Muslim or Hindu, it still hurts the same. When government hospitals treat patients worse than animals, the religion of the patient doesn't matter. When 90 per cent of Indians cannot afford fresh fruit because of inflation, it isn't just one community that feels the pinch. We all do, and it is time we ask our leaders to fix the problems rather than create new artificial ones.

I want to urge the Muslims of India to keep the heat on politicians. Don't commit your vote or loyalty to any political party indefinitely. Time has shown that they will only take you for granted. One should keep one's vote floating, and in the end, vote for the better—or less worse—party. Your vote has much more power if it can change over time.

The above, however, still doesn't take away the fact that our minority communities face oppression in some form or the other. Laws should be put in place to prevent discrimination and culturally, we will have to become more open-minded if we dream of seeing our country as a developed nation.

We are at a unique point in India's history. A significant part of the population is craving for change. Vote bank politics and hating the other's religion should be branded un-Indian. After all, our religions have stood the test of time. It is our nation, yours and mine, that has to be made great now. Are you on board?

Getting Realistic about Real Estate

'Didn't we get rid of feudalism when we achieved independence more than sixty years ago?'

A six-acre plot in Wadala, located in central-east Mumbai, was sold for an astronomical sum. Wadala is an upcoming but not a particularly posh area. The stunning price was possible because of the floor space index (FSI), allowing the builder to go vertical and sell as much as twenty times the area of the land plot.

In separate news, in August 2010, our Parliament passed the Salary, Allowance and Pension of Members of Parliament (Amendment) Bill, which hiked MPs' salaries from Rs 16,000 a month to Rs 50,000 and doubled some of their key allowances. Indian MPs are underpaid, compared to their global counterparts, or when compared to the level of talent required in terms of intelligence, leadership and professionalism. They make far less than the civil-service officers who report to them, which makes little sense.

However, despite the fact that MPs get less cash in hand compared to others, our lawmakers and the rest of the government administration are not exactly a low-cost proposition. This is due to the opportunity cost of the biggest dead asset they sit on—land. In Lutyens' Delhi alone, there're potentially a thousand acres of land occupied by bungalows, MP residences, various offices and quasi-government entities. Additionally, we also have dozens of 'think tanks' occupying super-prime real estate. These think tanks presumably add enlightenment to our society, though it is difficult to pinpoint even one or two solid contributions they have made in the past few decades.

Anyway, whatever their purpose, I am not proposing that we shut them down. All I am saying is that we, respectfully, move a portion of government housing, non-essential government offices and the think tanks out of super-prime areas to places like Gurgaon or Noida which are considered part of the National Capital Region. The move doesn't mean that the MPs have to slum it (and they won't, we know that). The new government complexes can be state-of-the-art, air-conditioned, Wi-Fi-enabled buildings. The residences can be luxurious in size and construction too. We can have personal statues of each MP in every room of their house if they want. And along with the move, MPs can get the pay hikes they have been demanding.

Of course, our lovable think tanks can also have new buildings with fountains outside where they can sit and scratch their heads all day and do ... I am sorry, not do anything but think. They can do this in Gurgaon or Noida just as well as in Delhi. I'm sure being next to Golf Links and Khan Market, like at present, is not particularly conducive to thoughts of social welfare.

To do a conservative cost calculation, an acre-sized bungalow in Lutyens' Delhi sells for around Rs 100–150 crore. A thousand acres, even at the low end of the range, is Rs 1,00,000 crore. Slap on a big FSI and the number can go up by ten times. Even conservatively, at half the amount, we arrive at Rs 5,00,000 crore. This is the blocked capital cost of running our wonderful government where MPs claim to make a pittance. Anyway, a complex in Gurgaon to replace this entire setup, with modern housing, offices—and the fountains for the think tanks—is unlikely to cost more than Rs 20,000 crore, or only 4 per cent of the blocked capital. The remaining amount can be used to reduce our staggering government debt. This, in turn, would lead to the country saving enormous actual cash interest costs every year. (If the Rs 4,80,000 crore of debt is reduced, we can save at least Rs 40,000 crore of interest costs every year.)

These are just the possibilities in Delhi. Similarly, every state capital has enormous government land in prime areas, reserved for sub-productive uses. The surplus railways and defence land is at another level altogether. If all that capital is released, the Indian government finances will finally begin to look healthy. The dreaded inflation, a common Indian problem, will also come under control.

There are other benefits of offloading real estate as well. There is something wrong about a government servant and his family living in a massive two-acre bungalow, costing Rs 200 crore, in a low-income democracy like India. It reeks of colonialism and has no place in the twenty-first century. Another benefit would be the development of new areas where the new offices and residences would be located. Newer construction also means more high-tech buildings that will improve government efficiency. The move will also release land, thereby easing pressure on real estate prices as well.

Of course, some caveats apply. Certain heritage buildings need to be protected, and should be. However, plenty of land will still be left, and not every old building can or should be preserved. To keep harping on heritage beauty at the cost of running a high-deficit, high-inflation economy is silly, unsustainable ostentation. If it prefers, the government can offer long leases rather than sell outright—the Wadala land sale was also a long-term lease. Environmental damage, of course, should be minimal.

One could argue against the practicality of this move, but if there is a will, it is partially doable. Frankly, doing this is far more practical than running an around-7-per cent inflation economy, which makes the poor and the middle class spend their lives chasing inflation and never able to accumulate real wealth. To sit on assets at the expense of the common people is called feudalism, and we were supposed to have ended that sixty-five years ago. This move could be inconvenient for the lawmakers for a while, but not impossible. Most importantly, it will be good for the people. After all, our politicians are meant to serve us, right?

India's Democratic Princes

> 'We need performing princes rather than ones for show.'

One of the reasons why India is unable to progress at a faster rate is because we simply don't have a mechanism to get the best person for the most responsible jobs in the country, especially in the political arena. Why are we like this? Why do we think that it is almost all right for a politician's son to become the next leader? I think there are three main causes. First, emotional decision-making. Apologies for stereotyping, but Indians are emotional people. The content of our films and TV programmes is ample evidence of this. When it comes to choosing a public figure, the decision is almost never completely rational. We are fond of Big B, so we give Junior B a chance. These things don't matter much when all you're doing is choosing the star you want to watch on screen. But it has huge repercussions when choosing people to run the country.

Political choices by voters must be rational. I am not suggesting that everyone with lineage will not be able to do a good job. Rahul Gandhi has resurrected the Congress. He speaks well, has kept his patience and not jumped to take the top post. Maybe those should be the reasons to elect him, but not because he reminds you of his father. Similarly, if some of his policies regarding subsidies are damaging the country's finances, you can consider switching your vote. Your vote is an important choice for your country, not an expression of love.

Second, there is a lack of institutions to groom political talent. We create great engineers and doctors but we don't take our liberal arts courses seriously. A handful of colleges are good, but most places are poorly run. We don't have any institutions like the Georgetown University in the US, for example, which actually trains students for political careers. The content of existing courses is outdated. I have met few political science graduates who can give insightful views on the current state of Indian politics and how to bring about change in the present times. Even apart from education, our political parties have no induction methods of taking in bright young workers, conducting training programmes or having a meritocratic evaluation system in place to make sure the best talent gets a chance to shine.

In the absence of all this, parties depend on a few charismatic personalities to run the show and their sudden absence creates a void which needs to be filled by a personality clone rather than the best leader available. This further acts as a demotivating factor for capable people to make a career in politics as they know they'll never make it to the top. And this, in turn, worsens the supply of good people in times of need.

Then there is the lack of political awareness. While we do study the oversimplified definition of a democracy in school—of the people, by the people, for the people—millions of Indians, particularly those in the economically weaker sections of society, still do not understand the full power of a democracy. Our history of monarchy is difficult to shake off, as democracy is a recent arrival in India's story. The established lines created by the caste system over centuries make it difficult to grasp the concept that anyone with talent can and, importantly, should, rise to the highest levels in society. In this scenario, we see political leaders as kings and their little princes are automatically next in line.

If we do pay attention to these issues, we can make the beginning towards building a robust political system that elects strong leaders who can take India to the next level. Meanwhile, the little princes should learn a lesson from Bollywood. Your pedigree may have given you a break, but you still need to perform. There are only so many flops daddy's name can support. Somebody may have made you a prince, but to stay there and become a real hero, you need to become a leader. The lights and cameras are on you now, so let's see if you can deliver. Action!

Ready for a Spring Cleaning?

'Do we want our children to mop up the mess we'll leave behind, or should we do it ourselves, now?'

Several Congress ministers have been accused of corruption. The 2G scam was a particular highlight. The Congress should do more than pay lip service to the notion of thoroughly getting rid of corrupt politicians. It is not enough to stop with outing a few and the occasional high-handed utterance, for by now the average Indian is wholly disgusted by the dishonesty that has permeated political life. Media hammering of scams has finally penetrated the consciousness of the man on the street.

In fact, scams have become quite entertaining to watch on TV. They have provided content to channels. None of the viewers believe that the accused leader is innocent. Yet, it is fun to see them defend themselves using almost any possible excuse—from the slow court system to the classic 'but everyone else is doing it'. It is gripping reality

TV—the confident smiles and swaggers of the accused, even as the world sees evidence of their guilt. Of course, the best part is the defiant 'why should I resign?', a sure sign that they will, very soon. It is reminiscent of the Iraq information minister who was on TV proclaiming an Iraqi victory even as American tanks rolled by right behind him. He was the most entertaining part about the Gulf War.

Yes, the Congress's defensiveness has indeed made things worse for them. The more it denies accusations, the longer the news story survives, the more fun it is to watch and the higher the TRPs climb, until, finally, the scamster ant is fried in the magnifying glass of the media glare.

So aren't resignations enough to douse the flames of a media story? That's the best that used to happen before, in the old India we grew up in. This time, though, it isn't enough. Take this example: A murderer shoots a man. When caught, he offers to surrender the gun. Or rather, he offers to give the gun to his best friend. Now isn't that how Indian politicians are punished? To give another example, a man batters his wife. When caught, he offers to leave the room. Is this how he will reform? Is this how to send a strong message to future wife-beaters?

Resignations used to be pacifiers stuffed in old India's face as it watched the government PR agency called Doordarshan. Things have changed. The media is on fire. The young generation knows the difference between lip service and real punishment for crime. And they communicate with each other far more than the previous generation. If the ruling party doesn't punish the guilty, the resignations will actually backfire.

To show it means business, the Congress would have to take three difficult steps. One, it needs to proactively classify its leaders, internally, as honest or corrupt. Two, it should rejig its power structure, perhaps through a portfolio reallocation, and give power to honest leaders. This is hard and will need a lot of backing from the top. Three, once power vests with the honest lot, they can take severe action, at least against the most visibly corrupt. This can be a 'reputation restoration' opportunity. The Congress could make cleaning India of corruption its mission.

However, if the Congress finds this too tough, maybe it would be wiser to give up power altogether so that the party can come back clean to fight another election. Staying in power is a privilege, but a burden, too. An injured weightlifter has to put down the weights, recover, and then lift them up again. To hold on to power with the help of corrupt partners is not a safe bet anymore. Every scam-artist minister is a time bomb waiting to explode.

Finally, a word for the opposition. It is doing the right thing by going after corruption. But it should not slam the entire Congress party on every occasion and should move from the slander-fest to a solution. It should focus on punishment for the guilty. Just as a terrorist has no religion, a corrupt politician has no political party. That is the attitude one needs. If all the political parties, the media and we, the citizens, play our roles right, we can spring clean our country. Let's leave a better India for the next generation so that their children say scams were something their grandfathers used to talk about.

The Silly Season

> 'The next time we have an election,
> do we express our prejudice, or shed it?'

Like certain flowers that blossom only in spring, Indian politics comes alive in its true colours only during election time. The strategies adopted by the political parties tell you what matters to people—how exactly do Indians vote? Certain moves announced by political parties for the 2012 UP election, whether absurd, controversial or unethical, provided immense insight into what works for the average voter. Even the most rational, modern-thinking politicians adopt primitive and regressive measures to pander to the electorate. They do this for one and only one purpose—to win. In fact, victory becomes so important that they forget or ignore the long-term repercussions of their actions on our society and nation as a whole. Take two examples, one each from the major parties, to see how peculiar Indian politics truly is. The first is the BJP's attempted induction of Babu Singh Kushwaha who had been rather publicly fired for corruption by the ruling BSP. The move backfired immediately and dented BJP's anti-corruption stance. While the media bashing forced the BJP to withdraw, the reason why the BJP did it wasn't pure stupidity. The Kushwaha community, classified in the OBC category, comprises nearly 10 per cent of UP's population. It is understood that the community votes en bloc and can cause a major swing in electoral fortunes. The controversy regarding his firing had made Kushwaha a star overnight. Such a tantalizing slice of UP's vote bank pizza was too much to resist. And even though the slice caused BJP much indigestion, one can understand the temptation.

The second, equally if not more, disturbing act was the Congress's proclamation of a Muslim quota within the OBC quota. Congress leaders went around UP publicizing their plan to extract a slice from the OBC quota for Muslims.

Both the actions had a devastating impact on Indian society and scarred Indian values. The first act implies that sins like corruption can be pardoned if you belong to the right caste. It says that we as Indian people don't value honesty above community. The impact of the second act, the Muslim reservation, is even more sinister. It divides Hindus and Muslims further. It sanctions privilege and advantage on the basis of religion. Religious reservations are bizarre. Consider this, one cannot convert his or her caste, but can convert their religion. So, could we see a scenario in the future in which a Hindu boy cannot get a job or college admission, but if he converts to Islam, he can get it under the quota? Are we incentivizing conversion? How can we allow such a policy to be even announced or be put in a manifesto, let alone take effect? The sad part is, such reservation does little for Muslims who need good education, entrepreneurship and empowerment to rise in society. Many Muslims are national icons in this country, and they have done it with their own talent, grit and determination. Muslims need an environment that nurtures their talent, rather than meaningless poll-time freebies. If a father gives his children toffees instead of buying books for school, it may get the child excited. But will you call him a good father? However, for a change, I am not blaming any of the politicians for the above two actions. Perhaps if we were in the same situation, we would be left with no choice but to adopt similar measures. The problem is not with the politicians, who simply mirror and adapt to the environment. The issue is with the Indian electorate, us. The great Indian mind is filled with prejudice. Centuries of persecution, discrimination that continues even to the present day, and a belief that one's own kind is superior has led to these prejudices. These in turn have led to a haphazard democracy that is more cacophony than consensus. The ruckus we often see in Parliament is nothing but a visualization of the average Indian mind, of chaos and confusion about who we really are. Even the most educated among us are prejudiced. One simple test of prejudice is this—will you allow your siblings or children to marry outside your community or religion? If your answer is no, then no matter how much you cheer for the Indian team, stand at attention for the national anthem or cheer the Indian flag—you are prejudiced. And until such time that most of us stay prejudiced, we will have the confused and mediocre leadership that we have right now. No matter how many fasts activists undertake, or good policies economists suggest, if in our minds we don't get the concept of being Indian, and treat that above anything else, we will remain a messed up country. Yes, dalits were treated badly in the past and some still suffer. Muslims were and some of them are still discriminated against. However, things have improved, and if you shed your prejudices, they will improve even faster. If there were no prejudice, there would be no need for the BJP to take in a tainted Kushwaha, and no need for the Congress to announce quotas within quotas. If we don't change however, we are going to move towards disaster. There will be lack of decision-making, inefficiency and a stalling of progress and growth. The young generation will find it even more difficult to get a good education and jobs. After all, if we choose our leader based on the toffees he gives us, then we deserve our fate. But all is not lost. The next election will bring us yet another chance—do we express our prejudice, or shed it. The choice is ours.

The Return of the Brash Politician

> 'Silence is no longer golden; politicians must start talking now.'

An interesting trend is beginning to become visible in the politics of our country— the rise of the assertive and aggressive politician. Most of India's high-profile former and current chief ministers—Narendra Modi, Nitish Kumar, Jayalalithaa, Mayawati, Mamata Banerjee, Sheila Dikshit—who have had spectacular victories, are vocal, opinionated and seem to have the 'let's get on with it' attitude.

This is in stark contrast to the stereotypical Indian leader who keeps quiet or, when forced to talk, is diplomatic to the point of avoiding the issue altogether. This stereotype emerged from the Congress party, which has successfully used the silent mystique strategy particularly well in the last twenty years. However, it may be time for such leaders to reconsider it, especially if they want to have a few rock star chief ministers of their own and be more in sync with what the Indian voter wants. Because, quite frankly, brash is back.

The classic example of the silent leader is P.V. Narasimha Rao, who was rarely heard from during his five-year prime ministerial tenure. It wasn't like he led India in boring times. India's near bankruptcy, economic liberalization, the Babri Masjid demolition and, of course, corruption scandals, were just a few of the big moments in his tenure. Yet, ask anyone who was around then—do they even remember his voice? After him, Sonia Gandhi has almost acquired a sphinx-like stature with her silences and her demure refusal to take up the prime minister's job. And, of course, Prime Minister Manmohan Singh is hardly known for his aggression or oratory. Don't talk, don't react, don't explain, don't take any opinionated stance—all this seemed to work extraordinarily well. Except, it doesn't seem so effective now.

This is India 2012 and silence is no longer equated with dignity, poise or high stature. So low is the credibility of politicians today that silence is seen as smugness, inefficiency and avoiding important issues. This is a cultural shift brought about by the frustration people have felt with unaccountable governments. From once-revered silent leaders, people have started to prefer brash assertiveness, even a bit of cocky confidence.

Such shifts in preferences do happen. In the US, it

is said that George Bush, often ridiculed as a not-so-sharp president, was a reaction to the 'extra-clever and glib' Bill Clinton. Americans were happy with someone less smart as long as he didn't get into scandals like his predecessor. Similarly, Indians today are more likely to give a brash politician who will speak a chance, rather than someone dignified who won't talk to the people.

There are lessons in this for all political parties. What worked in the past may not work so well in the coming few years. Whoever is positioned as a leader needs to have an agenda, a point of view, drive and, most importantly, a willingness to talk to people about issues. One doesn't have to react to every baseless allegation or news story. However, one must be willing to talk proactively on issues that are relevant to the people. Uttering platitudes or speaking in government officialese doesn't count. Statements like: 'We are examining the matter and in due course we will take a suitable course of action' are nonsensical. Be a straight shooter, come to the point, be honest about what you can and cannot do, and don't be afraid to have opinions.

We have had enough of posturing and need aggressive leaders. Political parties should ensure that the candidates they select have the required traits to suit changing voter preferences. Better start talking before people stop talking about you forever.

How to Reverse the Trust Deficit

'Are we sending the right people to Parliament?'

Anna Hazare managed to spur one of the most unapproachable governments in the world to positive action. He lit a desire for change among young people. He also started the much-needed process of restoring good values in Indians. Yes, many of us are still corrupt, whether forced by the system or otherwise, but a part of us yearns to be good. That part just became stronger. This mass booster shot of morality is the biggest contribution of the Team Anna movement, apart from the Jan Lokpal Bill.

Of course, these achievements did come at a cost. We saw a relatively long period of unsettling turmoil. We saw ugly, unpleasant qualities like stubbornness, insolence and over-aggressiveness from both sides on public display. In an ideal world, people would be reasonable and, irrespective of their position or power, do the right thing. However, we live in a far-from-ideal world and, given the circumstances, we came out relatively unscathed. This time, our youth did not come out on the streets to hurt people from another caste or religion. They came to simply demand a more fair and just society in a peaceful manner. It is a proud moment for all of us. India's current generation is different, and a salute to that.

However, I was shocked and disheartened by the intense criticism of Anna from certain sections of the English-speaking intellectual circles. If the elite had backed Anna more strongly, we could have had a quicker and better consensus. Of course, people have a right to an opinion. However, I often found that the opinions seemed more like a generic negative bias towards Anna, perhaps because of his rustic background, methods or sudden rise to fame which were all irrelevant to the issue at hand.

The strongest anti-Anna argument was that Parliament cannot and should not be subverted. There is no doubt that Parliament and the Constitution are important and have to be respected. However, these work on a basic assumption—confidence of the people. If confidence in them is lost, the institution does not work. And that is what we have to restore in Parliament now before we ask people to respect it.

How important people's confidence is, is illustrated by the following example. The paper notes we carry in our pocket have value only if people believe they have value. In many instances, people have lost faith in a country's currency. This normally happens when the government prints money without care, thereby devaluing it at a rapid pace, such as in Zimbabwe. At one point in 2008, prices were doubling in Zimbabwe every twenty-four hours. The profligate government printed money in higher denominations. The price of a loaf of bread reached 10 billion Zimbabwean dollars. Eventually, people dumped the currency and switched to a barter system. Now imagine, if elite Zimbabwe intellectuals came on TV and said that the monetary system of the country, the government and their currency must be respected above all. Would anyone have bought the argument? I don't think so. Steps to restore confidence were needed at the time. The government needed to commit that they would print money responsibly and put checks and balances in place. Zimbabwe didn't. People there now use foreign currencies.

Similar is the nature of the confidence crisis with politicians in India, particularly the government. Their constant lying has only made it worse. They keep saying corruption needs to be fixed, but do little. Even the prime minister uses the excuse of 'coalition compromises'. What is the compromise? On the truth, isn't it?

Lying is something politicians have gotten away with for a long time. It came at the cost of losing people's trust. A good Lokpal Bill will actually restore trust in the government. In fact, the government needs a Lokpal Bill almost more than the people need it. The government also needs to be more open and approachable. Party spokespersons need to have personal conviction and place what is right above the party, even if it means accepting mistakes.

And while we love telling politicians how to do their job, we, as citizens, have to do our bit to restore confidence as well. As I keep reiterating, we can't vote for candidates only because they are from a particular caste, religion or region. We have to consider only one criterion—is he or she a good person? When we all send capable, honest people to Parliament, trust and respect will return.

India on the Streets

'We have no hope if we cannot prove
Uncle Cynic wrong.'

We all have that one uncle who keeps reminding us how terrible India is. He tells us about how every government authority takes bribes—from the RTO to the ration shop to the municipality. He explains how no government department does its job well—potholed roads, abysmal conditions at government schools and poor healthcare are examples to support his theory. It is hard to argue with him, for he is right. Things don't work. There is no justice. Power talks. Equality doesn't exist. All of the above, even though uncomfortable to hear, ring true.

However, Uncle also goes on to say: 'Nothing will ever change.' He is convinced that our society is damaged irreparably, and India is destined to live in misery. Uncle Cynic doubts almost everyone, assumes the worst in people, and brands anyone who is trying to improve the country as someone with a hidden agenda.

This is where I think Uncle gets it wrong, horribly wrong. For it is one thing to point out the problems, it is quite another to give up trying to fix them. Cynicism is not a counter-argument; it is an attitude. For the fact is, we still have good people in the country, in society and even in government departments. It is just that they are crushed.

I don't want to give you the reasons why you must support Anna Hazare. It is almost beneath Anna's dignity that he actually has to beg or make a case for support when he is fighting for you against an abusive, corrupt regime. Still, let me do a quick recap of the facts.

Anna sat on a fast in April 2011 which became the nation's movement and spread virally. Concerned, the government agreed to make a strong Lokpal Bill, shook hands with the activists and, in principle, agreed to Anna's version which was designed to truly check corruption. Since then, the government has insulted Anna's team, thrown away their draft and come up with its own, almost pointless draft of the Lokpal Bill, which was passed in the Lok Sabha but hit a roadblock in the Rajya Sabha.

The draft the government presented to Parliament will not check corruption. Only 0.5 per cent, or one in 200 government officials are under its purview. Your corrupt ration shop, RTO, passport office, panchayat or municipal authority will not be covered. State scams will not be covered. The prime minister is excluded as well. How you ever heard of an anti-corruption law in a democracy that only applies to a certain section of people?

The government threw magic dust in our eyes and counted on India's illiterate and ignorant to not know the difference. However, you, reading this, are educated. You know when a wrong is committed. You know that while you have lived your life dealing with corruption, you do not want your children to do the same. A weak Lokpal Bill may not affect you today, but tomorrow it will hit you when your child does not get a college seat, when your hospital gives shoddy treatment, when your government work doesn't get done. We live in a poor country—poor, not because we don't have what it takes to be rich, but because our leaders have let us down. We have given them too much power, and they consider our vote a mandate to steal and be incompetent. They hate accountability. However, without accountability, our progress will stall. There are countries where the average income per person is fifty times more than in India. Don't we deserve the same?

Thus, whatever your personal view on Anna, it is not him but his cause that needs support. Anna did not create an anti-corruption sentiment, he merely tapped into it. Crushing Anna will not take away that sentiment, it will just make it fester more. Right now, the movement is still controlled. But the government needs to be careful about the way it acts. By being high-handed and going back on its word, it could send the country spiralling into chaos.

Finally, for the people of India, it is time to prove Uncle Cynic wrong. There is a bigger truth than his 'nothing ever changes in India'. That truth comes from the Gita which states: 'Nothing is permanent.' The Gita also says, 'When the pot of sin overflows, something happens to restore order.' Now it is up to you to determine if the pot of sin has overflowed. It is for you to say what it means for Indians to act out their dharma. And you, and only you, will decide if it is time to come out on the streets.

In Defence of the PM

> 'Money spent on bullets gives no returns;
> money spent on better infrastructure does.'

On the one hand, our relationship with Pakistan appears to be improving. On the other, we seem eager to ensure that we never regain a balanced relationship. When our PM talks to his Pakistani counterpart there are unseemly rows in Parliament and vociferous criticism in the media which appears ready to scuttle any moves either side wants to make to normalize the relationship.

Our attitude shows we really don't want to reconcile with Pakistan. Sure, we'd like relations to be better but deep down, there is resentment and anger. More than anything else, we want to teach Pakistan a lesson. We want to put them in their place. Bashing Pakistan is considered patriotic. It also makes for great politics.

We may feel our PM should not have spoken to them before resolving the Mumbai terror attacks case. However, let me tell you this, whether we talk to Pakistan or not, we are extraordinarily involved with them. We can cut off all contact; our leaders can exchange dirty looks with theirs and pretend they don't exist. However, every single Indian's future is linked to Pakistan and we all pay our dues in keeping the fight going. The reason is our defence budget. This is the most expensive item the government spends on, a fair bit of which is on account of Pakistan.

For patriotic reasons, defence expenditure is never questioned. After all, how can you question spending money on soldiers who give up their lives for us on the border? However, the bigger question is, did they have to give up their lives in the first place? And the second issue we need to understand is, for the amount we spend on defence, what are we giving up?

Yes, there is idealism in saying, 'We must have a strong army.' However, we are a poor nation. When you are poor, you need to be practical too. I think all Indians must have a rethink about three areas before we arrive at a consensus on our defence strategy.

Foreign Policy

Our foreign policy document is not a statement of national ego. It is a document that should articulate how we can best use our relationships with the outside world for the benefit of the country. Forget politicians, I want to ask my fellow Indians, how badly do we want Kashmir? At the cost of making colleges for the young generation in the country? At the cost of not doing irrigation projects for our farmers? At the cost of not building roads and power plants? At the cost of living in high inflation forever? Because, even though it may not be obvious, these items are linked. The budget for defence is more than all the above items put together. Our government doesn't have unlimited money, so what's better? Keep the fight going and prevent progress—or do what it takes to make peace, and use the money to build a stronger nation? The foreign policy document can play a big role in that.

Strategic Defence Alliance

The new globalized world has interlinked economies like never before. Nobody does anything all by themselves. We can have an alliance with another nation if the aim of defence is to protect our borders. For instance, America has a big need to ensure safety of its own borders and cut global terrorism. We can work with them—yes, by giving them some access to our country. For us, it can save costs in protecting ourselves. For them, they have better control over a volatile region. We may shudder at the presence of American involvement in our defence, but frankly, what advantage could they gain against us if they help us protect our borders? In this technology-driven age, do you really think America doesn't have the information or capability to launch an attack against India? But they don't want to attack us. They have much to gain from our potential market for American products and cheap outsourcing. Well, let's outsource some of our defence to them, make them feel secure and save money for us. Having a rich, strong friend rarely hurt anyone.

Good Old-fashioned Peace

The land of Buddha and Gandhi seems to have lost its goals for peace. We want to talk to Pakistan but more to put them in their place and shove our point of view down their throat. Frankly, such defiance may win claps from an audience in a cinema hall, but is no attitude for peace. We may think Pakistan is always wrong and we deserve Kashmir, but when we are in a negotiation, we have to give the other party some room. We may not be happy about it, but we can learn to live with it.

We need to have peace not only because it is a good thing, but also because we can't afford to fight or stay prepared to fight for the next twenty years. We are hiring more security guards outside the house when there isn't money to put the kids in school. The defence budget has to be controlled and with the right policies and attitudes, we can. Money spent on bullets doesn't give returns, money spent on better infrastructure does.

Let's Not Confuse Peace with Love

> 'We must give peace a chance for the nation to progress.'

Successive Pakistani regimes have done little to stem terror attacks that originate from Pakistan. Neither has Pakistan come out with any practical suggestions to the Kashmir problem. And still, in a naïve and almost spineless manner, we keep coming up with peace initiatives while they almost never initiate any such effort from their side.

The points may be valid and a case can be made for us to remain hostile towards Pakistan. However, while it is a tough call, the case for peace is still stronger. And sometimes in life, it is about taking the better option even if it doesn't appear to be macho. If making peace with Pakistan will give Indians a better life than hostility will, then we have to keep trying for the former option.

Let's see some basic numbers. The combined defence budget of the two countries is around $40 billion, of which over three-quarters is spent by India. This money is spent year after year. Compare this to the Golden Quadrilateral Highway Project, one of the major infrastructure projects completed by our government. The Golden Quadrilateral cost around $10 billion over five years and created more than 5,000 kilometres of roads that can be used forever. Where would you rather we spend our money? If peace efforts can bring military expenses down, isn't there an economic value for peace as well?

Hence we need peace not just because it is the morally right thing to do, but also because it is practical. We need peace because people with limited resources should not spend those resources fighting with each other. And yes, we need peace more because we have a good thing going in India and we have more to lose. There is nothing weak about it.

And while defence expenses have to be made, one should also realize that both sides are nuclear powers. In such a scenario, no matter how much anyone spends on defence, no one side can claim the ability to truly overpower the other. Both of us have that deterrent we'd never want used. Shouldn't rationality prevail at some point?

I must add that many peace-opposers also misunderstand peace. Partly due to the Woodstock-era associations of peace with love, people confuse that keeping peace with Pakistan means having affection for them. No, most of us who want peace want it because we love India, and not because we love Pakistan. Peace is not a free-hugs campaign or a touchy-feely warm and fuzzy feeling. Sometimes, peace is just boring indifference—or simply a desire to live and let live. And that's okay.

Once the case for peace is made, the next argument is, how can we do it without any intent from our neighbours? Again, the point is valid. However, to even hope for any initiatives from the other side, there needs to be democracy in Pakistan. Pakistan's democracy has come in fits and starts, often with leaders who are hardly reliable. However, under military rule, peace initiatives from their side are almost impossible. Peace challenges the raison d'être of the Pakistani army and hence they'd never dream of anything but pointing guns at their favourite enemy—us.

Therefore, India can campaign for a strong, viable democracy in Pakistan in a more aggressive manner than before. This can help tap into public sentiment there, which would also prefer self-governance. Such overt support to a democratic movement will weaken their military and improve India's image amongst the Pakistani people. Of course, this is not an overnight process. But efforts must begin soon if we want Pakistan to be stable enough so that it doesn't interfere with India's progress in the coming years. Immediately though, we can, as a democratic nation, refuse to engage with military governments and lobby against such regimes elsewhere. We have, in the past, expected to hammer a peace solution with Pakistani leaders who came to power by pointing a gun at someone. That, retrospectively, was a bit naïve.

Meanwhile, let's not give up hope for a peace that comes from indifference at least, and cut down hate because hate never led to anything good. Peace has clear benefits, particularly for India's younger generation, who'd rather see more opportunities for themselves than more wars.

Finally, just because peace efforts are difficult, we can't be sceptical about them. Attempts at peace may or may not be successful, but if nobody even tries, there won't be any hope. After all, as John Lennon said in the iconic song, 'All we are saying is give peace a chance.'

OUR YOUTH

India is the youth. This is something you will hear often, mainly because India's median age is twenty-five, and 70 per cent of the population is below thirty-five. However, despite these claims, the youth have little say in mainstream politics or national issues. The youth are under-represented. This is mainly because the Indian youth is not a vote bank. I have often been decribed as one of the voices for the youth of the nation. I am not sure if that is correct, but I do try to speak about youth issues wherever possible. Young people read my books, mostly, and I want to do something for my readers.

In the youth of India I see hope for change. I see them as impressionable, open to ideas and willing to accept that things need to be different. It is from the youth that I derive most of my optimism.

In 'We Don't Need No Education', 'Indian Institue of Idiots', and 'The Bootlegging of Education', I talk about the Indian education system, one of the causes I am deeply passionate about. In an 'Open Letter to Sonia Gandhi from Young India', I try to imagine what the youth might say to the most powerful person in the country. In 'Letter to Bapu from Generation Next', a young person writes to Gandhi, talking about the current situation.

As you read this section, I am sure you will gain more empathy and appreciation for the plight of the Indian youth which works hard at every stage to secure a good education and career.

My Stupid Suicide Plan

'If God wanted us to take our own life, he would have provided a power-off button.'

We come across, unfortunately with great frequency, many reports about student suicides, especially students belonging to our elite institutions. People who commit suicide do it because they feel they have no future, nothing to live for. But wait, isn't IIT the one place where a bright and shining future is a foregone conclusion? It just doesn't add up, does it? Why would a young, hardworking, bright student, who has the world ahead of him, do something like this? The answer is this—in our constant reverence for the great institution (and I do believe IITs are great), we forget its dark side. And the dark side is that the IITs are afflicted by the quintessential Indian phenomenon of academic pressure, probably the highest in the world.

I can rant about the educational system and how it requires serious fixing, or I can address the immediate problem—try my best to prevent such suicides. I have chosen the latter, and I do so with a personal story.

News of a suicide always brings back one particular childhood memory. I was fourteen years old when I first seriously contemplated suicide. I had done badly in chemistry in the class X half-yearly exam. I was an IIT aspirant, and 68 per cent was nowhere near what an IIT candidate should be getting. I don't know what had made me screw up the exam, but I did know this: I was going to kill myself. The only debate was about the method. Ironically, chemistry offered a way out. I had read about copper sulphate, that it was both cheap and poisonous. Copper sulphate was available at the local kirana store. I had it all worked out.

My rationale for killing myself was simple—nobody loved me, my chemistry score was awful, I had no future and what difference would it make to the world if I was not there? I bought the copper sulphate for two rupees— probably the cheapest exit strategy in the world.

I didn't do it for two reasons. One, I had a casual chat with the aunty next door about copper sulphate, and my knowledgeable aunty knew about a woman who had died that way. She said it was the most painful death possible—all your veins burst and you suffer for hours. This tale made my insides shudder. Second, on the day I was to do it, I noticed a street dog outside my house being teased by the neighbourhood kids as he hunted for scraps of food. Nobody loved him. It would make no difference to the world if the dog wasn't there. And I was pretty sure that its chemistry score would be awful. Yet the dog wasn't trotting off to the kirana store. He was only interested in figuring out a strategy for his next meal. And when he was full, he merely curled up in a corner with one eye open, clearly content and not giving a damn about the world. If he wasn't planning to die any time soon, what the hell was I ranting about? I threw the copper sulphate in the bin. It was the best two bucks I ever wasted.

So why did I tell you this story? Because sometimes the pressure gets too much; as happened with the students who took their lives. And when they took that dreadful decision, all the lives that were linked to theirs were shattered and India lost wonderful, bright children. And as the silly but true copper sulphate story tells you, it could happen to any of us or those around us.

So, please be on the lookout. If you see a distressed young soul, lend a supportive, non-judgmental ear. When I look back, I thank that aunty and that dog for unwittingly saving my life. If God wanted us to take our own life, he would have provided a power-off button. He didn't, so have faith and let his plan for you unfold. Because no matter how tough life gets and how much it hurts, if street dogs don't give up, there is no reason why we, the smart species, should. Makes sense, right?

Sparks[*]

> 'I come from a land of a billion sparks;
> isn't that cool?'

Good morning everyone and thank you for giving me this chance to speak to you. This day is about you. You, who have come to this college leaving the comfort of your homes (or in some cases discomfort) to become something in your life. I am sure you are excited. There are few days in human life when one is truly elated. The first day in college is one of them. When you were getting ready today, you felt a tingling in your stomach. What would the auditorium be like, what would the teachers be like, who are my new classmates—there was so much to be curious about. I call this excitement the 'spark' within you that makes you feel truly alive. Today I am going to

---

[*]This is a speech I gave at an orientation programme for MBA students in Symbiosis, Pune, on 24 July 2008. I hope it will help you too.

talk about keeping the spark shining. Or to put it another way, how to be happy most of, if not all, the time.

Where do these sparks start? I think we are born with them. My twin boys have a million sparks. A little Spiderman toy can make them jump on the bed. They get thrills from creaky swings in the park. A story from daddy gets them excited. They do a daily countdown for a birthday party—several months in advance—just for the day they will cut their own birthday cake.

I see students like you, and I still see some sparks. But when I see older people, the spark is difficult to find. That means as we age, the spark fades. People whose spark has faded too much are dull, dejected, aimless and bitter. Remember Kareena in the first half of *Jab We Met* versus the one in the second half? That is what happens when the spark is lost. So how to save the spark?

Imagine the spark to be a lamp's flame. The first aspect is nurturing—to give your spark the fuel, continuously. The second is to guard against storms.

To nurture, always have goals. It is human nature to strive, improve and achieve one's full potential. In fact, that is success. It is what is possible for you. It isn't any external measure, a certain cost to company pay package, a particular car or a house.

Most of us are from middle-class families. To us, having material landmarks is success and rightly so. When you have grown up in a country where money constraints force everyday choices, financial freedom is a big achievement. But it isn't the purpose of life. If that was the case, Mr Ambani would not show up for work. Shah Rukh Khan would stay at home and not dance anymore. Steve Jobs wouldn't be working hard to make a better iPhone, as he would have Pixar for billions of dollars. Why do they do it? What makes them come to work every day? They do it because it makes them happy. They do it because it makes them feel alive. Just getting better from current levels feels good. If you study hard, you can improve your rank. If you make an effort to interact with people, you will do better at interviews. If you practice, your cricket will get better. You may also know that you cannot become Tendulkar, yet. But you can get to the next level. Striving for that next level is important.

Nature designed a random set of genes and circumstances from which we were born. To be happy, we have to accept it and make the most of nature's design. Are you? Goals will help you do that. I must add, don't just have career or academic goals. Set goals to give you a balanced, successful life. I use the word balanced before successful. Balanced means ensuring your health, relationships, mental peace are all in good order.

There is no point of getting a promotion on the day of your breakup. There is no fun in driving a car if your back hurts. Shopping is not enjoyable if your mind is full of tensions.

You must have read some quotes—Life is a tough race, it is a marathon or whatever. No, from what I have seen so far, life is one of those races in nursery school. where you have to run with a marble in a spoon kept in your mouth. If the marble falls, there is no point coming first. Same with life, where health and relationships are the marbles. Your striving is only worth it if there is harmony in your life. Else, you may achieve the success, but this spark, this feeling of being excited and alive, will start to die.

One last thing about nurturing the spark—don't take life seriously. One of my yoga teachers used to make students laugh during classes. One student asked him if these jokes would take away something from the yoga practice. The teacher said—don't be serious, be sincere. This quote has defined my work ever since. Whether its my writing, my job, my relationships or any of my goals. I get thousands of opinions on my writing everyday. There is heaps of praise, there is intense criticism. If I take it all seriously, how will I write? Or rather, how will I live? Life is not to be taken seriously, as we are really temporary here. We are like a pre-paid card with limited validity. If we are lucky, we may last another fifty years. And fifty years is just 2,500 weekends. Do we really need to get so worked up? It's okay, bunk a few classes, goof up a few interviews, fall in love. We are people, not programmed devices.

I've told you three things—reasonable goals, balance and not taking things too seriously which will nurture the spark. However, there are four storms in life that will threaten to completely put out the flame. These must be guarded against. These are disappointment, frustration, unfairness and loneliness of purpose.

Disappointment will come when your effort does not give you the expected return. If things don't go as planned or if you face failure. Failure is extremely difficult to handle, but those that do come out stronger. 'What did this failure teach me?' is the question you will need to ask. You will feel miserable. You will want to quit, like I wanted to when nine publishers rejected my first book. Some IITians kill themselves over low grades—how silly is that? But that is how much failure can hurt you. But it's life. If challenges could always be overcome, they would cease to be challenges. And remember—if you are failing at something, that means you are at your limit or potential. And that's where you want to be.

Disappointment's cousin is frustration, the second storm. Have you ever been frustrated? It happens when things are stuck. This is especially relevant in India. From traffic jams to getting that job you deserve, sometimes things take so long that you don't know if you chose the right goal. After books, I set the goal of writing for Bollywood, as I thought they needed writers. I am called extremely lucky, but it took me five years to get close to a release. Frustration saps excitement, and turns your initial energy into something negative, making you a bitter person. How did I deal with it? A realistic assessment of the time involved—movies take a long time to make even though they are watched quickly, seeking a certain enjoyment in the process rather than the end result—at least I was learning how to write scripts, having a side plan—I had my third book to write and even something as simple as pleasurable distractions in your life—friends, food, travel can help you overcome it. Remember, nothing is to be taken seriously. Frustration is a sign that somewhere you took things too seriously.

Unfairness—this is hardest to deal with, but unfortunately that is how our country works. People with connections, rich dads, beautiful faces, pedigree, find it easier to make it—not just in Bollywood, but everywhere. And sometimes it is just plain luck. There are so few opportunities in India and so many stars need to be aligned for you to make success happen. Merit and hard work is not always linked to achievement in the short term, but the long term correlation is high, and ultimately things do work out. But realize, there will be some people luckier than you. In fact, to have an opportunity to go to college and understand this speech in English means you are pretty damn lucky by Indian standards. Let's be grateful for what we have and get the strength to accept what we don't. I have so much love from my readers that other writers cannot even imagine it. However, I don't get literary praise. It's okay. I don't look like Aishwarya Rai, but I have two boys who I think are more beautiful than her. It's okay. Don't let unfairness kill your spark.

Finally, the last point that can kill your spark is isolation. As you grow older you will realize you are unique. When you are little, all kids want ice cream and Spiderman. As you grow older and in college, you still are a lot like your friends. But ten years later and you realize you are unique. What you want, what you believe in, what makes you feel, may be different from even the people closest to you. This can create conflict as your goals may not match with others. And you may drop some of them. Basketball captains in college invariably stop playing basketball by the time they have their second child. They give up something that meant so much to them. They do it for their family. But in doing that, the spark dies. Never, ever make that compromise. Love yourself first, and then others.

There you go. I've told you the four thunderstorms—disappointment, frustration, unfairness and isolation. You cannot avoid them, as like the monsoon, they will come into your life at regular intervals. You just need to keep the raincoat handy to not let the spark die.

I welcome you again to the most wonderful years of your life. If someone gave me the choice to go back in time, I would surely choose college. But I also hope that ten years later as well, your eyes will shine the same way as they do today. That you will keep the spark alive, not only through college, but through the next 2,500 weekends. And I hope not just you, but my whole country will keep that spark alive, as we really need it now more than any moment in history. And there is something cool about saying, I come from the land of a billion sparks.

We Don't Need No Education

> 'Citizens should be the strict teachers who will tell leaders they have a lot of homework to do.'

HRD ministry statistics demonstrate a significant decline in national primary school enrolments. Given Indian demographics, where the number of children is increasing every year, the results are even more shocking. This despite all the noise made about right to education for every Indian. While we may choose to forget this statistic for the next sensational news item, this is an extremely disturbing development.

If India's population is not trained to face the globalized world—and primary education is the first step in that training—we will become a nation of servants and clerks. And going by the almost constant firefighting most our leaders, to cover up scams do rather than promote education, it doesn't seem likely that our top leadership cares. Still, if enough citizens care, maybe politicians will take notice. It is with this hope that I will try to analyse the possible reasons for this decline, what will happen if we don't address it and what we can do to actually fix it.

There are five main reasons why enrolment could have dropped. One, the most obvious reason, is that the schools are terrible. If you ever visit a village school, you will realize how everything is of low quality, from the classrooms to the desks to the quality of teachers. Why? Don't villagers deserve good schools for their children? One may say the schools are subsidized, so quality cannot be maintained. Well, maybe we need to spend more money then. Maybe we need more private partners. Maybe we need to redesign the traditional model of a school, perhaps using technology to impart learning. The education may be at the primary level, but it still needs to be of high quality. Low-quality education is not really education at all.

Two, the curriculum in our schools is obsolete. How much has the professional world changed in the last thirty years? How much has our curriculum changed? Who sets our curriculum? Do they revise it from time to time, keeping in mind the needs of the industry and the services sector? One big reason poor people send their kids to school is so that they can learn skills to make more money. If schools don't give them those skills, why will they bother? Advanced concepts like education to satisfy curiosity, or learning for learning's sake, do not apply to people with no money. A hungry person does not watch Discovery Channel. Surveys show that a person with decent English language skills can increase earning power by 400 per cent. Why don't we teach our people English? Why do government schools start teaching it so late?

Three, the massive inflation rate has made life extremely difficult for people with low incomes. Every pair of hands on the fields is now more valuable than sending a child to a substandard school for several years, the benefits of which are unclear.

Four, there isn't enough money being put into education to make more schools or improve existing ones. Tax collections have seen high double-digit growth rates for several years now. However, much of taxpayers' money is used to fund scams and mass bribery-type subsidies or to pay interest (often on borrowings made to fund past budget extravagances). If the 2G auctions had been done properly, or the Commonwealth Games hadn't wasted so much money, we could have had a lot more schools. If, instead of NREGA, we provided villagers the right skills to enhance farm income and increase job eligibility, maybe we would generate wealth rather than burn it.

Five, a controversial, sinister reason: the hidden benefits of illiteracy to politicians. Illiterate people are useful when it comes to maintaining vote banks and keeping scam parties going. If everyone was well-educated, would the government get away with so many scams? The politicians keep saying, 'People vote for us, hence our actions are justified.' If every Indian really understood what happened, could the loot continue? So while there may not be a deliberate strategy to keep people illiterate, there is no burning passion or political incentive to make India educated either. And politicians only work on incentives, not out of the goodness of their hearts.

This problem won't go away. It will get worse. If today millions aren't being educated well, how will they get proper jobs tomorrow? Won't the education crisis translate into a far scarier job crisis in a few years? Or are we happy for our kids to remain poor forever?

This can be fixed. Primary education has to be vast enough in scale and scope to be seen as a utility such as power or telecom. The most modern techniques, thinking, strategy and execution are needed on a massive scale to educate our people. Ideally, just as with a few power utilities, the effort should be privatized, maybe on a semi-subsidized basis. In any case, if the education is worth it, people pay for it.

Course materials have to be brutally revamped to bring them in sync with the modern world. Rural schools need Internet connectivity even more than big-city ones. These are things we should demand from the leaders of our country. They don't seem to care much. But we, the citizens, have to be the strict teachers who tell our leaders that they have a lot of homework to do.

Learn and Share English Lessons with All

> 'Hindi is our mother, English our wife, and it is possible to love both.'

China may soon have more English speakers than India. These findings come from the British Council study, 'English Next India' by David Graddol. This has startling implications. Command over the English language is seen as one of the few relative advantages we had over China. I reviewed the study and found it more important (and far more readable) than the much talked about, but obsolete, Lieberhan Report and other pointless documents our government dishes out—and the media passionately reacts to—on a regular basis.

The desire for English in India is underestimated. English is not a trend, a fad or an upmarket pursuit. English helps me face an interview, read the best academic books available and access the world offered by the Internet. Without English, progress for a middle-class youth is heavily stunted. However, the state of, and attitude towards English education leaves much to be desired.

Let's talk about the state first. There is a tiny minority of English speakers who are extraordinarily fluent in the language, probably more than most Britons. That tiny minority also means millions of people in a country as large as India. These people had parents who spoke English, had access to good English-medium schools—typically in big cities. They then gained proficiency early on, which, in turn, helped them to consume English language products such as newspapers, books and films, thus increasing their command over the language. English is so instinctive to them that even some of their thoughts are in this language. These people, the E1s, if I may call them that, are much in demand. Irrespective of their graduation specialization, they can get frontline jobs across various industries—hospitality, airline, media, banking and marketing.

However, apart from the E1s, there are a large number of E2s, probably ten times the number of E1s, who are technically familiar with the language and even understand it. However, their English communication is not at a professional level. If they sit for an interview conducted by E1s, they will come across as incompetent, even though they may be intelligent, creative hardworking. They cannot comfortably read English newspapers and are thus denied the chance to upgrade their language skills. They know English but have not been taught in an environment that facilitates this virtuous cycle of continuous improvement through the consumption of English language products. Thus, while the difference in the level of an E1 and E2 may not be too different at age ten, by age twenty, it is so stark that an E1 can get many jobs while an E2 won't even be shortlisted for many. For lack of proper teaching, an entire world is closed to the E2s. After the E2s, there are people who don't have access to English at all. These people need to begin with basic learning. However, E2s constitute an amazing number of youth across the country who just need that extra push to take them to the next level.

I've sat with the management of over fifty colleges, many in smaller towns. I distinctly remember an MBA college in Indore. The principal, an IIT graduate, told me, 'My biggest concern is that my students don't know how to speak proper English. Sometimes I wonder, should I teach them finance and accounts or should we just take basic English grammar classes. For, during interviews, no matter how well they can analyse a company, they will not be comfortable putting a sentence together. What were their schools doing? And why should a postgraduate MBA college be doing this?' That said, he hired ten teachers for his 200 students for the sole job of teaching them proper, MNC interview-ready English.

To convert the E2s to E1s, a complete overhaul of the English school curriculum is required. We can't count on the teachers alone as we simply don't have enough good ones. We must give students, even the senior secondary ones, simple, relevant and fun English course materials that they enjoy reading, watching or learning from, so that they get into the self-driven virtuous cycle of consuming English language products. Forcing them to read antiquated or convoluted books, because some PhD in literature classifies them as good, is the same as giving a primary school student a Nobel thesis in the name of science. It will scare the child and kill any curiosity for further exploration. This is a fixable problem, and I hope the SCERTs and NCERTs are going to pay attention to address it.

Apart from the state of the English language, the second hindrance is the attitude. There are two attitudes—first, the snobbery. A section of people believe that teaching and learning English should be a high-class affair. Elitism and English are linked and people who speak good English look down on people who don't. Elitism hurts the inclusion process and without inclusion, the nation as a whole can never progress.

The second attitude arises when English is seen as a threat to Hindi or other local languages. It is not, but this needs to be communicated with sensitivity. Local languages are neglected and we must do more to support them. However, that is a separate issue. English is not competing with the vernacular—but it is a necessary skill for middle-class youth to rise in the modern world. Hindi is your mother, English is your wife and it is possible to love both at the same time.

As a developing nation, English is one of the few tools available to make Indians take their rightful place in the world. Let's make sure we keep it sharp and share it wide.

Indian Institute of Idiots

'Our education system is crying out for a revamp.
When will we get around to doing it?'

I avoid writing on the Indian education system as it is not good for my health. For days, my blood continues to boil, I have insomnia and I feel like hurting someone real bad. The Indian education system is a problem that can be fixed. It affects the country's future, impacts almost every family, everyone knows about it and it is commercially viable to fix it. Still, nothing happens because of our great Indian culture of avoiding change at all costs. Because change means sticking out your neck and that, ironically, is something we are taught not to do.

There are two main problems: one, the supply of good college seats and, two, the actual course content and intent behind education.

The first issue is about the supply of A-grade institutions versus the number of A-grade potential students. With one crore students taking the class XII exam each year,

119

the top 10 per cent, the high potential population by any global standard, deserve a world-class institution. That means, we need 10 lakh good, A-grade, branded college seats per year. Either the government provides them or they work with private participants to make it happen. Until that is done, the scramble for seats will be worse than a peak-hour Virar fast. No amount of well-meant advice to parents to go easy on kids, to children to not take stress, will work. I'm sorry, if I have a child who I think is bright, I will fight to make sure he gets into a good college. If the number of seats is well below the required amount, the fight is going to be bloody and ugly. And that is what happens every year.

What makes me most curious is why the government doesn't fix it? Real estate and faculty are often the biggest requirements in creating a university. The government has plenty of land. And any advertisement for government teaching jobs gets phenomenal responses. After this, there are running costs. However, most parents are happy to pay reasonable amounts for their child's college. With coaching classes charging crazy amounts, parents are already spending so much, anyway. Indians send $7 billion (over Rs 30,000 crore) as outward remittance for Indian students studying abroad. Part of that money would be diverted inwards if good colleges were available here. The government can actually make money if it runs universities and add a lot more value to the country than, say, by running the embarrassing Air India which flushes crores down the drain every day.

Why can't Delhi University replicate itself, at four times the size, on the outskirts of Gurgaon? The existing professors will get more senior responsibilities, new teachers will get jobs and the area will develop. If we can have kilometre-long malls and statues that cost hundreds of crores, why not a university that will pay for itself? This is so obvious that the young generation will say: duh!?

The education system's second problem is the course content itself. What do we teach in school and college? And how much do you use it in daily life, later? Ask yourself, has the world changed in the last twenty years? If yes, has our course content changed at the same pace? Has it even changed at all? Who are the people changing our course materials? Do they have real-life corporate exposure?

I am not saying that we study only to get a job (though many, many Indians actually do so with that main intention). However, even in the 'quest for knowledge' goal of education, our course materials fall short. We emphasize sticking to the course, testing endlessly how well the student has revised his lessons. We treat lessons as rules to be adhered to, and the better you conform, the more likely you are to score. I hated it personally and I am sure millions do, too, but they have no choice. Innovation, imagination and creativity, crucial for the country, as well as more likely to bring the best out of any student, have no place in our education system. In fact, we actually ensure we kill this spirit in the child as fast as possible. Because innovation by definition means challenging the existing way and that is just not something good Indian kids who respect elders do.

The cycle perpetuates itself and we continue to create a second-rate society of followers rather than change-embracing leaders. I have hope that the current generation will break this norm and start questioning the great Indian way. I have hope that the current HRD minister will acknowledge this problem and do something. I have hope that Indians will start questioning any politician they meet on what they are doing about the education system at every place possible. I have hope that people will realize that making new states is less important than making new state universities. Maybe I am right, maybe my hope is justified, and maybe I will live to see the change. Or maybe I've got it all wrong, my optimism is misplaced and I am just, as they say, one of the Idiots.

The Bootlegging of Education

'The no-profit policy in private
education is stupid.'

Many well-meaning people, including the director of IIT Delhi and software guru Narayana Murthy, have commented about the flaws in our higher education system. Their comments reflect a general concern about India's institutions of higher learning.

Barring a tiny percentage of elite colleges, higher education in India is of questionable quality. Ask corporate honchos, and they will talk about a serious shortage of talent. Ask students, and they will say there are no good jobs. Clearly, students are not being trained properly to meet the demands of the globalized world.

Almost everyone agrees that something needs to be done about the education system. Strangely, little is done about it. Money spent on education is never questioned; it isn't really a politically divisive issue and fixing it is a matter of a few right policies and reforms, unlike far more complicated problems such as corruption.

We have good, reputed colleges that, at best, accommodate 10 per cent of the applicant pool of students. What happens to the rest? Obsessed with starting salaries, IITs, IIMs and DU cut-offs, we ignore the millions that don't make it. Where do these students go? Do they have a shot at a good life?

Many of these students end up in private colleges. These private colleges have played the role of providing students with a chance to earn a degree of their choice. There is nothing wrong with this. It fact, it is even good that the private sector is playing a role in educating our students. But the quality of these institutions is an issue.

Thousands have opened up in the last decade. In the NCR region alone, there are over a hundred MBA colleges now. With such proliferation, quality standards vary widely. While there is a demand for them, given our large student pool, what they are teaching and what students are learning is another matter. To ensure quality, the government has put in place procedures like elaborate approval processes and regular inspections. However, these are abused and corruption is rife. Many private college owners have personally admitted to me that they had to pay bribes at every stage of setting up the college— from getting land and building approvals to approving the course plan and setting fee structures. Corruption in the private education sector is such a norm that nobody in the know even raises an eyebrow anymore.

One big reason for corruption is the government's no-profits-allowed policy for private institutes. Every educational institution has to be incorporated as a non-profit trust. Technically, you cannot make money from the college. The government somehow believes that there are enough people who will spend thousands of crores setting up good colleges for the millions who need seats every year just out of the goodness of their hearts. On this flawed, stupid assumption that people are dying to run colleges without ever making money rests the higher education of our country.

Of course, none of this no-profit business ever happens. What happens is that shady methods are devised to take money out from the trust. Black money, fake payments to contractors and over-inflation of expenses are just a few ingenious methods to ensure promoters get a return on their investment. This means that none of the legitimate players ever enter the field. Ex-academics, world-class corporate houses and honest people will never touch private education for they do not want to pay bribes at every stage and devise shady methods to bypass no-profit rules. Thus, people like country-liquor barons, sari manufacturers and mithai-shop owners open technical colleges for engineering and medicine. And we hand over our kids and their future to them.

You don't need to be an expert to realize that what is happening is seriously wrong. However, policymakers are doing little about it. Perhaps, much like the bootlegging industry, so many regulators and inspectors are making money that nobody wants to fix the problem. However, corruption in the education sector is not to be taken lightly. When you have corruption in infrastructure, you have potholed roads. When you have corruption in education, you have potholed minds. We are destroying an entire generation by not giving it access to the world-class education it deserves.

I have nothing against commercialization of education. Commerce and business are good things. However, when it comes to education, a sense of ethics and quality is needed. Good people must be incentivized to open colleges. Say, by a simple policy fix, like allowing private institutes to make a profit. This would mean that companies like Infosys and Reliance might open colleges, perhaps on a large scale, as shareholders will approve the huge investment required. If these companies open colleges, at least they will be of a certain standard. If the business model is sustainable, many good players would be attracted to this sector.

This can be done. This *needs* to be done. Indians care about education. We can have one of the best education systems in the world. It is a matter of collective will and a few good leaders to make this happen. It should not require a fast or dharna or yatra or anti-politician slogans. When something is sensible, it should just be done. For that is what educated people do. And we would like to call ourselves educated, won't we?

Letter to Bapu from Generation Next on His Birthday

> 'India, for which you gave your life, is still far from free.'

Dear Gandhiji,

You left us more than sixty years ago. If you were still around, you would have been more than 140 years old. However, we have not forgotten you. You are on every banknote and most stamps. There are many statues of you. Prestigious roads in almost every city are named after you. Our politicians try to model themselves on you. They wear the fabric you promoted, they quote you at every instance, they've got a photograph of you in their offices and some even eat and live like you. There are books, TV programmes and movies about you. Seriously, you'd be impressed at how much we still adore you.

However, there are things that won't make you feel proud. The India you spent all your life making free is far from free. True, the white guys are gone. But there are still millions of poor people. After sixty-plus years, we are still among the poorest nations on earth. This lack of money leads to a lot of problems in healthcare, infrastructure and education. Many children still don't go to a good school. Those who do don't get into good colleges. And those who go to college don't get good jobs. We need to get rich, and fast. Not only to make more schools and colleges, but also because most Indian problems are linked to the lack of money. Yet, it is considered un-Indian to think that way. The young generation, which thinks like that, is considered materialistic and greedy. The older generation takes the moral high ground—slowness in work is termed patience, non-stop discussion and no action is called careful consideration and lack of improvement in standards of living is countered with claims about the need to live with austerity. And yes, in many cases, politicians who speak like this claim to be your fans.

The younger generation wishes you could come down for one day and clarify these points. Is progress un-Indian? Is change bad? Is a desire to see my country as rich as some other nations materialistic? Is getting things done fast impatience? If you blessed our purpose of building a developed India, the job would become so much easier.

The young generation needs you down here for something else, too. We have a new battle here, just like the one you fought with the British. The enemy is not as clear as it was in your case—the white people. Our enemy is the old school of thought, or rather, the people who defend the old school of thought. They do this in the name of antique Indian policies, culture and values. You could help identify this enemy more clearly. Many people who are at the helm of affairs now have served India for decades, maybe with good intentions. But obviously they don't want to accept they screwed up. We wish they would, though, and we'd have a national day of shame. It won't be easy, but from there we could make a new beginning. But they won't, for they are in power. And to defend themselves and their ways, they don't mind crushing the aspirations, ideas and talent of an entire generation.

Yes, there is a lot of talk of India being a young nation and about youth power. However, youth power is the biggest myth going around India right now. Of course, the youth has spending power—we can buy enough SIM cards, sneakers and fizzy drinks to keep many MNCs in business. But we do not have the power to change things. Can the youth get a new college set up? Can the youth ask the government to provide tax incentives to MNCs to relocate jobs to smaller towns? No way. We are wooed, used, but seldom heard. If you came down, you could unite us. You used religious festivals as social events and propagated your cause. You understood that people need entertainment to bind them. Perhaps we could integrate colleges in the same way, link all colleges—maybe for their annual festivals—and the message of change could be channelled through them. We have amazing technology, such as the Internet, now. You would use it so well. If the youth unites, there could actually be youth power.

With our purpose blessed, enemy identified and youth united, we could take the first steps towards the new Indian revolution. After all, China had one and only after that did they get on the path of true progress.

But if it is not feasible for you to come back, we'll have to try to bring about change ourselves. If we can be inspired to do that, we can say we have not forgotten you and understand the meaning of your birthday. We hope you had a good one up there!

Lots of love,
The Younger Generation

When It's Crass versus Class

'Big fat displays of wealth are so uncool!'

'Is that a snake, Daddy?' my then five-year-old son asked me, when he saw on TV a giant garland made of rupee notes around a politician's neck, Surely my son wasn't making a profound comment on the implied symbolism of what materialism stands for in society today. After all, the garland did actually resemble a snake—a python that slowly suffocates its prey to death. The human ATM that that politician had turned into will certainly hold its place among the over-the-top things rich Indians regularly do to inform others of their wealth.

While the money-snake was in a different league, one only has to see how affluent people in this country conduct their weddings and birthday parties to realize how deeply we want to scream to the world: We have the cash! After all, what is the point of having money if your relatives, colleagues, neighbours and even random strangers don't know you have it?

I once heard of a birthday party where all attending kids were given Nike Air sneakers as return presents. I've attended birthday parties with life-size Cinderella carriages and faux Formula One car racing tracks laid out for four year olds.

There is a show on TV called *The Big Fat Indian Wedding,* on which rich families allow television crews to cover their weddings. In the only episode I could bear to watch, the wedding functions were spread over a week in Delhi, Rajasthan and Bali, with 500 guests being shuttled around. At the end, like every wedding, only one boy and girl got married.

An international newspaper had a front-page story, this time about a village in Noida. A farmer made a killing selling land to developers, and hired a helicopter for his son's wedding in the village.

An argument can be made defending such behaviour: if someone has earned the money, he or she has the right to do whatever they want with it. We should be happy Indians are finally coming into money. So if someone wants to give a politician a money-python or a money-elephant, what is anyone else's problem?

Yet, at one level, it just doesn't feel right when I see my kids witnessing vulgar displays of wealth. Because here's the message running in my child's head: this is what successful people do. This is what life is all about. I'm asked to work hard so that one day I can make money, smear my face with cash and burn money to tell the world I've arrived.

Displays of wealth diminish values like self-control and being down-to-earth, humble and sensitive. Winners inspire the young generation. The loudness created by money dwarfs the contribution made by other people in society—teachers, honest cops and doctors, to name only a few—who may not be as rich, but are still good role models for children. For this reason, I'd like to request the country's rich people to hold their horses. Calm down, we know you have it. Put it on your website if you really want us to know how much money you have, but don't let it all hang out. We are impressed you made it, well done, 10 out of 10, bravo! Now let us be.

Not all rich people live like this. Warren Buffet, one of the richest individuals in the world, lives in a simple five-bedroom house in Omaha. One of the most respected figures in American society, he doesn't have to show off. In Silicon Valley, hundreds of self-made millionaires go to work in T-shirts and jeans. Flashing wealth is frowned upon. Crassness is not a necessary part of affluence. Grace, while seemingly still a new concept to rich and powerful Indians, is possible to learn.

This doesn't mean that wealthy people do not deserve their luxury. Surely they shouldn't have to slum it like the rest of us. However, there is a difference between private and public luxury. They can eat off gold plates and bathe in Evian water at home, if that is a source of satisfaction for them. However, when their wealth display goes public, they should think twice. If some politicians find inner joy in surrounding themselves with currency notes, it is tough to argue with that. They can wallpaper their rooms with 1,000-rupee bills (the Gandhi images will add a nice touch of irony to the decor). However, they don't have to wear million-dollar cash garlands and display it to Indian kids. Their sycophants, along with people who believe money equals greatness, may even admire and applaud them for it. However, there are some, if not many, of us who don't.

We don't want our kids to emulate such behaviour. We want them to emulate true leaders. Leaders who show excellence, benefit society and help people. Leaders who show restraint, poise and humility. Those are the people we can truly call rich. On the day the politician wore that hideous garland, she did not come across as rich. She came across as a helpless woman trapped in a bunch of notes, which threatened to strangulate her political career like a python.

Don't Fix
Look at the

> 'Don't ban books, just give us bette

Sometimes I wonder if television c_ politicians to enact drama in real life. Aft_ else can we have top leaders of a leading party _ many days discussing a historical figure, banning a_ and firing the author from a position he's held for th_ years. I have no ill feelings for the BJP (or the Congres_ party for that matter).

In fact, I'd like to see both parties being as strong as possible so that the Indian voter gets to choose between two really good alternatives. However, the slow-suicide path the BJP has chosen for itself is harmful not only for their party but for the nation. With no credible second alternative, a democracy runs the risk of turning into a one-party monopoly, which may not be good for the country in the long term.

ty is that despite its best intentions, the
f touch with the current generation. Take,
e, its ire over the book *Jinnah: India Partition
ce* by Jaswant Singh. The BJP screamed that Mr
as not as secular as claimed by Jaswant Singh.
on TV cited events in 1932 which proved that
was a good person. They were countered by an
number of experts who cited historical events to
e that Jinnah did terrible things.

To answer the Jinnah question from the point of view
the young generation—who cares?

Really, whether Mr Jinnah did wonderful things or
horrible things, the point of view of the party, etcetera—
who gives a damn? How is this relevant to the India we
have to build today? Are we electing leaders for the future
or selecting a history teacher?

The strange thing is that the media buys into pointless
debate and spends hours discussing it. By doing so, it gives
legitimacy to the whole exercise. Meanwhile, the young
generation fails to understand why our politicians become
so passionate about defending these relics of the past.
Why don't they have a passionate debate about how fast
they will build roads, colleges, bridges and power plants?
Why don't people get expelled over non-performance
rather than historical opinions? Why don't we ban useless
government paperwork rather than banning books about
dead people?

Every Indian student learns about past leaders. We read their biographies, celebrate their birthdays and see them as inspiration. However, what made these people great was the fact that they brought about change for a better future during their time. Do our politicians realize this before they claim to be fans and devotees of past leaders? Or is it simply easier to debate the past than to roll up your sleeves and make change happen. This old Indian mentality of non-stop discussion and no action has cost the nation dearly. If our political parties cannot find ways to change this quickly, they just might find themselves becoming irrelevant.

Open Letter to Sonia Gandhi from Young India

> 'You are, madam, best placed to change the things in India that need changing.'

Dear Soniaji,

I've never been much of a fan of open letters. After all, why make public something meant for one person? However, I don't have your email ID; you don't seem to be on Facebook (and certainly not on Twitter). Regular mail will never get past your sycophants. Hence, this seems to be the best option. Also, I don't speak only for myself. It's something a lot of young Indians currently feel. However, we don't know the right channel to express this and get it addressed.

The issue is simple: India must get rid of corruption. Whatever the solution, you will have a pivotal role in implementing it.

I don't think you would have a personal interest in being corrupt. Money would hold little significance for you. You don't come across as someone who aspires to a lavish lifestyle. Yes, the compulsions of running a political party require vast amounts of funds. This brings in cronies and moral compromises, which have become part of any Indian politician's life.

In recent times, however, there have been too many of these compromises. Amounts have reached levels that cannot be computed on a digital calculator. Scam after scam—and these are only the unearthed ones—show how we have created a monster of a system that rewards evil and threatens the dream of India becoming a 'first-world' country.

Recently, your son spoke about how corruption prevents the benefits of globalization from reaching the common man. This is absolutely true. In fact, it not only cuts existing benefits, it cuts out future opportunities for the young. Corruption is worse than terrorism. Terrorists blow up existing infrastructure such as roads, airports and power plants. Corruption prevents such infrastructure from being created in the first place. Terrorists take innocent lives. Corrupt politicians prevent hospitals from being built, which means that innocent lives that could be saved are not.

You say corruption is a disease. But that sounds a little defeatist. A disease is something inflicted upon us by nature. Corruption isn't caused by little bugs. Corruption comes from unchecked power. Take the example of electric power, a wonderful invention that brings light and comfort to our homes. But before this power reaches us, it is kept under control at various sub-stations to limit voltage and current. If electric power is unchecked, it can burn down our homes. Political power is unrestrained in India. Like little kings, our MPs roam around with their sycophants, blocking traffic, openly defying laws and doing anything and everything possible to exploit their power. If you want to fix this 'disease'—and you can do it—you need to pass a 'Political Accountability Bill' in Parliament. Also, an independent council against corruption needs to be set up. It should not be under the control of politicians and should have the power to prosecute politicians—almost all 'first-world' countries have this. Without these changes, no matter how many wonderful speeches are made, the disease will remain uncured.

Mechanisms to punish errant politicians are one aspect. It's equally important to understand why so many politicians err in the first place, and the reforms required to prevent that. Some of your party's ideas seem well intentioned—particularly the massive push to bring young people into politics. Your son has travelled across the country to spread this message.

But I want to ask—what happens when a young man joins the Youth Congress (or another party's youth wing)?

To do well, he will need to spend most of his energies serving the party. Parties do not have a formal stipend or salary system, so how is the young man expected to survive except through petty corruption? This is how a fine young man is forced to take small steps towards becoming corrupt. In such a scenario, would you advise educated, intelligent young people to join politics? Instead, if a proper stipend system were put in place, strong performers would have a mechanism to rise and contest elections and you would have a whole new class of talent in the profession of politics. Unless these reforms happen, including youth in our politics will be nothing but one of the specialties of our politicians—empty talk.

Other nonsensical rules in Indian politics include the Rs 25 lakh limit on electoral campaigns. The actual average spend, my MP friends tell me, is around Rs 6 crore per constituency. Where does this unaccounted money come from? Obviously, one stands little chance if one is not corrupt. Can we not remove these impractical and outdated limits? Why not define legitimate fundraising methods? If we do that, many good people would enter politics and change the face of this nation.

As a nation, we have enormous expertise in covering our backs and not rocking the boat. Right from school, Indians are taught to shut up and not question anything. Thus, even though some of the above issues are obvious, nobody important will sit up and say, 'We need to change things.'

It isn't easy to change things but it needs to be done. And you, of all people, have the best chance of taking this archaic bull by the horns and showing it the right direction.

The question hundreds of millions of young people are asking is: are you up for it?

Respectfully,
Young India

Where's My Nobel Prize?

> 'Talent is the most precious national resource; we must nurture it.'

Whenever a person of Indian origin wins a prestigious international award, especially the Nobel Prize, there is much hand-wringing at home. 'Why don't we win Nobel prizes here?' becomes the question of the week. The standard arguments are brought out: we don't have the facilities, there is too much government interference, the selection process is rigged, the prize committee is racist and, finally, who cares about the Nobel anyway? Of course we do, that's why we discuss it.

And then, like all news stories, the furore dies down, until the next time someone of Indian origin is feted abroad. However, maybe it is time to look at the core issue: why India doesn't excel on the world stage on a fairly consistent basis. We don't win a significant number of Olympic medals, we don't create global brands, our IT industry is essentially based on a job transfer model but we haven't created even one Google, Facebook or Twitter. (Of course, there is plenty for Indians to be proud of otherwise, so please don't jump on me because of my observations.)

The real issue comes down to the treatment of talent in our country. So what is talent? Talent refers to a special ability and aptitude that gives people an edge in a particular field. In sport, science, films, business or the arts, people who dominate the world stage all have a gift that makes it easier for them to excel. Of course, along with talent, there is preparation, hard work and a certain amount of luck required to achieve success. However, talent is usually a necessary ingredient. Talent is rare and randomly distributed across the human population, irrespective of pedigree, connections or wealth. Some may call talent an unfair gift. However, it is talent that allows ordinary people to come up in life. Otherwise, rich people would stay rich and poor people, poor. Thus, this unfair talent actually makes the world fairer.

However, we don't put talent on the highest pedestal in our country. A talented person's stature is below that of someone with connections, hereditary entitlement, pedigree or even experience. If I were to tell you that an unknown boy from Agra will become the next superstar, versus a star's son becoming the next star, the latter story is much easier to digest. Even in an IIT, a truly gifted young faculty member cannot jump ranks and scales set by the system. And the people designing the system never took talent into account. Even when talent is identified, we are unable to train it and find it difficult to reward it.

It is difficult to say why we have this attitude, but there are many possible reasons. One, talent conflicts with the traditional Indian caste system. Two, according to Indian cultural values, we revere the older generation and its experience, and talent zooms past it. Finally, the 'tall poppies syndrome', an already existing term used in Australia and the United Kingdom to 'describe a societal phenomenon in which people of genuine merit are criticized or resented because their talents or achievements elevate them above or distinguish them from their peers'. Ask yourself, have you seen some of this in India? Maybe because so many dreams have been crushed in India, someone else's success reminds us of our own failure. The US (only as a contrasting example; I'm not recommending that we become like them) has an opposite value system. Talent is respected, seen as something to be emulated. That is why they have teenage boy bands and college dropouts who open dotcoms, as national icons. We don't.

There are grave negative repercussions for a community that doesn't respect talent. It leads to a society where connected people do better than people with ability. It leads to a lot of talent being unused, a tremendous waste of a national resource. It causes frustration in the entire new generation, as they see people with less capability doing better than them. It also reinforces the old Indian values of fatalism and the helpless-common-man theory. And it means India's excellent people may not excel worldwide to the extent possible.

So what can be done? Well, we definitely can do something both at the macro organizational level and a micro individual level.

At the organizational level, we have to let go of corporate hierarchies and the lifelong promotion ladders of government, particularly in talent-dependent organizations like R&D, companies requiring high innovation or sport. We have to make incentives in line with what attracts talent, as there is a global battle for it. Exceptional talent demands exceptional reward. We have to take away the moral judgement associated with rewarding talent. Just as it is morally okay for a rich man's son to be rich, a person with talent also deserves to do really well.

Change needs to happen amongst us, at the individual level, as well. We have to acknowledge that talent exists, and we need to respect it. Frankly, isn't it better a talented person gets rewarded rather than a minister's undeserving son? Talent shouldn't cause resentment, it should become an inspiration. I think the young generation is already on board with that. It needs the older generation's support to make this change in values. It may be difficult, but it is worth it.

Because if we do become a talent-driven country, we will become a more progressive nation, utilize the new generation's skills properly, become a fairer society and, along the way, win a few Nobel prizes, too.

Save Us from the 'Lerds'

'The lerds and the nerds must join hands
to build a better India.'

There is a common, slightly insulting term used to describe certain people with a scientific or technical background—nerd. Nerds are defined as people slavishly devoted to academic pursuits. They are supposed to be intelligent but socially awkward, lost in equations and formulae and disconnected from the real world.

Not every person with a technical background is socially inept. However, I, being from the species, humbly accept there are enough nerds in this world to create the stereotype. Many of us find it easier to solve differential calculus than, say, speak to strangers at a party. I have been tagged as a nerd at various stages of my life, especially while being turned down by women (as in 'I'd prefer being a nun to being seen with a nerd like you' or 'go solve your physics problems, nerd, the Stephanian already asked me out').

I accept it. Sometimes it is difficult for nerds to articulate or absorb what is happening in the real world. Nerds like to solve problems and get quite uncomfortable if they cannot find the answer in a certain number of steps. Hence, it is relatively easy for a nerd to figure out how a rocket is launched into space, which, though complex, has a set, solvable path. It is much harder for nerds to approach questions like 'how do I get this girl to like me' or, more seriously, issues like 'how to solve corruption' or 'why is the Indian economy and politics in such a mess?'

I accept it; we, in our rigorous yet narrow-minded scientific education, find it difficult to approach subjective issues. That is why we are called nerds.

However, after accepting the flaws of my own species, allow me to point a tiny finger at our humanities-stream brethren. Allow me, ladies and gentlemen, to introduce a new, nerd-equivalent category for our 'liberal arts' background people—the lerds.

The lerds are our so-called 'liberal arts', or in India, simply the 'arts' students who are supposed to be open-minded, visionary and articulate about social issues. Some of these people, with their background in wonderful liberal arts subjects, are our intellectuals. They sit on think tank committees and participate in debates to solve issues facing our country. Lerds give forty-five-minute speeches in conferences held at posh Delhi venues on topics ranging from the environment, corruption to poverty eradication,

FDI, the girl child, healthcare and infrastructure. Lerds can be spotted in TV debates on English news channels (but never on entertainment or vernacular channels). Female lerds often prefer an ethnic yet classy look.

Unlike nerds, who shiver at the thought of public speaking, lerds can speak on any issue. When they do, they sound intelligent, even though their point is often not clear. Warm, fuzzy feelings run through their listeners as they see the lerds' grasp of issues like the primacy of Parliament and their use of wonderful terms like 'need of the hour' (notice the urgency. Not need of the week, month or year—need of the hour).

Lerds know it all. They understand nuances like a nerd never would. However, unlike nerds, who love solutions, lerds have one defining, important trait. Despite all their intelligence, grasp and knowledge, lerds hate solutions. For solutions mean that there is a direction set to solve the problem, and then there is not much debate left. And where is the fun in that? So, if a Lokpal Bill is proposed as a starting step to solve corruption, lerds will hate it.

Because, according to them, the 'need of the hour' is to remove corruption. However, how exactly that is to be done is not the lerds' concern. So if, for inflation, solutions like reduction in government subsidies and productivity improvement infrastructure projects are proposed, they will shoot it down with an 'it is not that simple' or an

'India is not that easy to figure out'. For, you see, all that lerds are interested in is to figure out the problem (and show the world how smart they are at figuring it out). Proposing or backing a solution is for plebeians and nerds. Lerds are above all this.

Where do lerds come from? Well, they are often a result of the flawed Indian education system which focuses on knowledge more than application. Even in science subjects, but particularly in the arts, Indian students can score good marks through rote knowledge, rather than being forced to apply themselves. Teaching materials and methods in the humanities are archaic and outdated. Many postgraduates in wonderful subjects like sociology, philosophy, psychology and economics have excellent knowledge, but find it difficult to apply their knowledge to the Indian context, and impossible to provide a specific solution to problems.

Of course, not every liberal arts student is a lerd (just as every tech student is not a nerd). However, it is time we accept that intelligent yet inept people exist on both sides—the sciences and the arts. Knowledge is only one part of education; the other, equally important aspect, is application. Nerds need to integrate their problem-solving abilities into the real world. Lerds need to learn how to solve problems, rather than just pontificate. Arts and science streams are just man-made divisions. To progress, we Indians need to learn and apply from both disciplines.

I hereby propose a truce between the nerds and the lerds, who should come together and learn from each other. After all, isn't that the 'need of the hour'?

Can Engineers Be 'Touchy Feely'?

'Let's find out if there is a heart behind the calculator at all.'

I remember the incident. I was in a restaurant and one girl in our group was especially charming. So I, like any other male, tried to put on a wooing act. You know the routine—a nanosecond extra eye contact, a few more nods to whatever she says and attempts to throw in those one-liners, which you know you wouldn't have said if she weren't there. And it seemed to be working. She leaned forward when she spoke to me, and every now and again, we'd have a small conversation of our own, separate from our group. She laughed at my approach with the fork and knife, and I teased her about her hairband, which had little teddy bears on it. Yes, we were flirting.

A while later, she asked me the question: what did I study? I said engineering, without any particular meaning attached to it. And then, like a cold metal rail, she went stiff. My jokes weren't funny anymore. Her eyes wandered to everyone else.

What was it? Why? Why? Why?

Two days later, I still couldn't get over the great start that had dissipated listlessly upon mentioning my education. Engineer? What was wrong with that? My mom had wanted me to become one since I was five! I had to call her. 'So what happened to you that day, hot-and-cold missy?' And then she said, trying to be nice, 'Well, it's just that I am sceptical about engineers as friends. I don't know, they can be, you know, very logical and everything...not very touchy feely.'

Not touchy feely. Now, what the heck did that mean? Well, she obviously did not mean it literally, since girls don't really suggest that sort of stuff, certainly not in the first meeting across the table. I guessed it had something to do with feelings, sort of having an emotional side. The stereotype being the nerdy guy who sees relationships like laws of physics, to whom love is just a bunch of chemicals going crazy in your brain and getting to know a person means obtaining their biodata.

It's time to set the record straight.

It's true that a lot of what engineers study—and they end up studying quite a lot—has to do with formulae, laws and numbers. No matter how hard we try, some of the vocabulary we read all day gets into our language.

So when my mother said, 'Are you getting married next year or not?' I ended up saying, 'Well, at this moment in time, the probability is relatively low,' and felt it was completely normal to say it. And when my sister went sari shopping and couldn't explain the shade she wanted, I told the shopkeeper the percentages of pink, orange and red in the sari.

Yet, ladies, I don't think we're bad at relationships, love and getting to know people. We, too, can be touchy feely, as that is part of our education as well. The reason for this is that most engineering students live through this 'touchy feely' thing. Relationships.

Imagine eating, sleeping, brushing your teeth, bathing—okay, rarely this one—and partying with the same people all the time. So when you are kicking that bathroom door down for the tenth time, or when you stand in line for gulab jamuns in the mess and when you are done with the vodka bottle and sharing all your secrets, you know it is good practice. Yes, hostels maketh the man. So, the next time you are in a flirtatious situation with the techno types, go on, flirt a bit more. Of course, I am biased towards my kind, but if you find the conversation turning too geeky, just ask them, 'So, what were your hostel days like?' and chances are, you'll see a heart behind the calculator.

Coming back to my missy, I thought of what would make me win her over. Flowers...too cheesy. Music...I don't know her taste (nor do I trust mine). Teddy bears...

don't even go there. Desperate for some good lines, I just turned it right back at her. 'Yes, I know what you are saying about engineers. The thing is, unless people with depth like you start hanging out with us, we won't get any better. Can you meet me some time for some touchy feely...oops, I mean coffee or tea?'

She giggled. When they giggle, it means you have won.

TWO SHORT STORIES

At times, fiction brings out issues and concepts with much more clarity and ease than non-fiction ever can. So in this section I am including two short stories. 'Of Ducks and Crocodiles' is an allegory about a two-faced government and 'The Cut-off' is a way to show the stress caused to students by ever-increasing university cut-offs.

Of Ducks and Crocodiles

Once upon a time, there was a beautiful village on a hill. The simple villagers worked hard on their terrace farms. Everything was perfect, apart from one problem: there wasn't enough water through the year. The rainy season was fine, but at other times, the villagers relied on a lake on top of the hill. In the rainy season, the hardworking villagers collected water in buckets and filled the lake. Once full, the village enjoyed the lake for the rest of the year. It was a good system and the village was set to prosper. The lake also became a wonderful picnic spot. It housed some beautiful ducks. The children from the village liked to come and watch them. The ducks often invited the children for a swim.

The villagers felt they owed their life to the lake. The ducks became like deities. In particular, there was a family of ducks with gold-tipped feathers. The villagers saw these golden ducks as a divine life source. When the villagers toiled to collect buckets of water to refill the lake, they chanted praise for the golden ducks.

Other ducks also followed the golden ducks. The golden ducks had appointed a wise duck—an old, intellectual-looking one—to stand at the centre of the lake. The wise duck barely moved, and the stillness added to his mystique. Villagers prayed to the wise duck as well.

Everything was wonderful. Sometimes, the golden ducks smiled at the villagers and everyone would go into an ecstatic frenzy. The wise duck always had the same expression, so it was difficult to tell if he was smiling or not.

One day, however, things went horribly wrong. Three children who had come to the lake for a swim went missing. People looked everywhere, but the children could not be found. The next week, two more children went missing. The villagers went to the only person they knew who could have an answer—the golden ducks and the wise duck.

However, the golden ducks didn't speak. The wise duck said something like, this can not happen in this village.

The next week, four more children went missing. One villager found body parts by the lake. It looked like someone had eaten the kids. The villager heard a rustle in the water. He could recognize the creature.

'There are crocodiles in the holy lake!' the villager screamed as he ran across the village square.

The villagers went into a panic. However, they could not believe it. They confronted the holy ducks again,

160

although apologetically, as they didn't like to disturb them so often. 'What are you talking about?' the wise duck said. 'We have no crocodiles. Other jealous villages have stolen our babies.' The wise duck, having said enough, limped away to swim on the other side of the lake. The golden ducks remained in their private cave.

Over six months, fifty children went missing. Some villagers pointed fingers at the lake, but the villagers called such people attention-seeking hacks and ignored them. The villagers felt that if the wise duck had said there were no crocodiles, there were no crocodiles.

One night, however, almost all the villagers heard a noise from the lake. Scared, they woke up and tiptoed there. They were stunned at what they saw. There was a grand party of crocodiles by the lake. They had all come out to feast, dance and lay new eggs. Some ducks danced with the crocodiles, too. The golden duck family remained in their private cave and the wise duck sat still at the corner of the lake.

'Oh, wise duck,' villagers rushed to him, 'what is this? You said there are no crocodiles.'

The wise duck seemed in pain as he spoke. 'You have to compromise sometimes,' he said.

'With people who eat our babies?' the villagers said. 'If you had told us early on, we could have killed the first few crocodiles. Now there are hundreds of them. Why, wise duck, why?'

Dawn broke even as the wise duck remained silent. After many months, it promised to be a sunny day. The sunrays came out, enabling one to see under the water clearly. The villager saw the wise duck's feet in the water. A strong set of teeth were holding them. Aghast, the villagers saw the set of crocodile eyes under the water. It swam away. The wise duck, legs stuck to the reptile's jaw, went along with him.

The villagers realized what was going on. Even the golden duck family had crocodiles outside their cave.

'Enough's enough, we have to do something ourselves,' the villagers said.

Over the next few months, they started to dig a new lake. They also made several mini-lakes at various levels of the terrace farm. They put strong iron meshes so the crocodiles could not enter. They collected buckets of water and filled it in the new lakes. One smart villager put an underground pipe to empty out the old lake and fill the new one. Soon, the old lake had no water. As it dried up, the crocodiles and ducks struggled to live. They begged the villagers for some water but the villagers paid no attention.

The new lakes opened, and the villagers loved them. They also realized that they had made the lake, and not the other way around. Children came back to swim in the new lakes, crops had enough water and the village prospered like never before. Everyone in the old lake died. And the villagers lived happily ever after.

The Cut-off

Everyone will give you an opinion on how to live your life. No one, no one, will give you good advice on how to end it. Worse, they will tell you to continue living, without any respect for individual choice. Yes, hi, I'm Gautam Arora, and after eighteen wonderful years in Delhi, I've decided to end my life.

I sat with my best friend Neeraj and his girlfriend Anjali at Costa Coffee, DLF Metropolitan Mall, Saket. The coffee was way overpriced, but considering I had a day to live, I didn't mind getting ripped off.

'The joke isn't that funny,' Neeraj said, tearing open the second sachet of brown sugar and mixing it for his girlfriend. If this girl couldn't mix sugar in her coffee, I wondered what she would be like after marriage.

'Do I look like I am joking? You are in medical college, and as a friend and someone two years elder to me, I am asking your advice on what is the most painless, graceful way to go. And ideally, it should be available at the friendly neighbourhood chemist,' I said. I ordered a chocolate fudge cake. What are a few extra calories on your last day?

Anjali kept quiet, her iPod plugged to her ears. She had come to the mall to shop with her boyfriend rather than meet me. Neeraj said he only dated Anjali as her father had given her a car and driver, which made it easy to get around. Besides, she looked okay. She was pretty enough to invite a second stare from men, though that's hardly an achievement in Delhi, where men's standards are quite modest.

'Dude, you topped your school. How much did you score in your class XII boards again?' Neeraj said.

'92 per cent,' I said.

'Ninety what?' Neeraj said as he ripped out Anjali's earphones. 'Anjali, the dude scored 92 per cent in commerce! Do you know of anyone who has scored that much?'

Anjali shook her head. 'Wow, you must have studied a lot,' she said.

I nodded. I had done nothing but study in the last two years.

'No time for hobbies?' she asked.

I shook my head. My only hobbies were eating three meals and sleeping five hours a day. The rest of the time was spent with my books.

'With ninety-two, you should be fine,' Neeraj said.

'Not according to SRCC, not according to Stephen's

and not according to Hindu...Oh what the heck,' I said as I opened my rucksack.

I gave him the special admissions supplement from the newspaper. I had snuck it out early morning so mom and dad wouldn't see it.

'Wow, check out Lady Shri Ram College. B.Com Honours is at 95.5 per cent!' Neeraj said.

'That's a girls' college,' Anjali said.

'I know,' I said.

'Don't worry, he wouldn't have made it anyway. Anjali, why don't you go spend some of your father's money,' Neeraj said and winked at me.

Anjali and I both gave Neeraj a dirty look. Neeraj air-kissed Anjali and gestured to her to leave.

'Seriously, don't kill yourself. To us, you are still the school topper,' Neeraj said after Anjali left.

'So what do I do?' I said, my voice loud, 'stay back in school? This topper tag makes things worse. My parents already threw a party for our friends and relatives like I have made it big time in life. I cut a cake on which the icing said "family superstar".'

'Nice,' Neeraj said.

'Not nice at all. All the relatives congratulated my mother. They see me as the next hotshot investment banker on Wall Street. The least they expect me to do is get into a good college in DU.'

'There are still some colleges that you will get into,' Neeraj said as I cut him off.

'But none with the same brand value. Thus, you can't get a decent job after them. You can't get into the top MBA school.'

Neeraj pushed my coffee cup towards me. I hadn't touched it. I picked it up and brought it close to my mouth but couldn't drink it.

'I made one tiny calculation error in my math paper,' I said, 'read one stupid unit conversion wrong. That's it. If only...'

'If only you could chill out. You are going to college, dude! Branded or not, it is always fun.'

'Screw fun,' I said.

'What kind of kids are they taking in anyway?' Neeraj said, 'you have to be a bean-counter stickler to get 97 per cent. Like someone who never takes chances and revises the paper twenty times.'

'I don't know, I revised it five times. That stupid calculation...'

'Gautam, relax. That paper is done. And sticklers don't do well in life. Innovative and imaginative people do.'

'That's not what DU thinks. You don't understand, my father has proclaimed in his office that I will join SRCC. I can't go to him with a second-rung college admission. It's like his whole life image will alter. Hell, I won't be able to deal with it myself.'

An SMS from Anjali on Neeraj's phone interrupted our conversation. *At Kimaya, tried fab dress. Come urgently, want your opinion.* Neeraj typed the reply back. *Honey, it looks great. Buy it.*

Neeraj grinned as he showed me his response. 'I think you should go,' I said. Rich dads' daughters can throw pretty nasty tantrums.

Neeraj took out the money for coffee. I stopped him. 'My treat,' I said. Leave people happy on your last day, I thought.

'Of course, I take this as your treat for cracking your boards,' Neeraj said and smiled. He ruffled my hair and left. I came out of the mall and took an auto home.

I met my parents at the dinner table. 'So, when will the university announce the cut-offs?' my father said.

'In a few days,' I said. I looked up at the dining table fan. No, I couldn't hang myself. I can't bear suffocation.

My mother cut mangoes after dinner. The knife made me think of slitting my wrists. Too painful, I thought, and dropped the idea.

'So now, my office people are asking me, "When is our party?"' my father said as he took a slice.

'I told you to call them to the party we threw for neighbours and relatives,' my mother said.

'How will they fit in with your brothers and sisters? My office people are very sophisticated,' my father said.

'My brothers are no less sophisticated. They went to Singapore last year on vacation. At least they are better than your family,' she said.

My father laughed at my mother's sullen expression. His happiness levels had not receded since the day I received my result.

'My office people want drinks, not food. Don't worry, I'll have another one for them when he gets into SRCC or Stephen's.'

My father worked in the sales division of Tata Tea. We had supplied our entire set of neighbours with free tea for the last five years. As a result, we had more well-wishers than I'd have liked.

'Even my country head called to congratulate me for Gautam. He said—nothing like Stephen's for your brilliant son,' my father said.

'Gupta aunty came from next door. She wanted to see if you can help her daughter, who is in class XI,' my mother said.

Is she pretty, I wanted to ask, but didn't. It didn't matter.

I came to my room post dinner. I hadn't quite zeroed down on the exact method, but thought I should start working on the suicide letter anyway. I didn't want it to be one of the clichéd ones—*I love you all* and *it is no one's fault* and *I'm sorry, mom and dad*. Yuck, just like first impressions, last impressions are important, too. In fact, I didn't want to do any silly suicide letter. When it is your last, you'd better make it important. I decided to write it to the education minister. I switched on my computer and went to the education department website. Half the site links were broken. There was a link called 'What after class XII?' I clicked on it; it took me to a blank page with an under-construction sign. I sighed as I closed the site. I opened Microsoft Word to type.

Dear Education Minister,

I hope you are doing fine and the large staff of your massive bungalow is treating you well. I won't take much of your time.

I've passed out of class XII and I've decided to end my life. I scored 92 per cent in my boards, and I have a one-foot-high trophy from my school for scoring the highest marks. However, there are so many trophy-holding students in this country and so few college seats that I didn't get into a college that will train me to get to the next level, or open up good opportunities.

I know I have screwed up. I should have worked harder to get another 3 per cent. However, I do want to point out a few things to you. When my parents were young, certain colleges were considered prestigious. Now, forty years later, the same colleges are considered prestigious. What's interesting is that no new colleges have come up with the same brand or reputation level. Neither have the seats expanded in existing colleges fast enough to accommodate the rising number of students.

I'll give you an example. Just by doing some meaningless surfing, I saw that 3.8 lakh candidates took the CBSE class XII exam in 1999, a number that has grown to 8.9 lakh in 2009. This is just one board, and if you take ICSE and all other state boards, the all-India total number is over ten times that of CBSE. We probably had one crore students taking the class XII exam this year.

While not everyone can get a good college seat, I just want to talk about the so-called good students. The top 10 per cent alone of these one crore students is ten lakh children. Yes, these ten lakh students are their class toppers. In a class of fifty, they will have the top five ranks.

One could argue that these bright kids deserve a good college to realize their full potential. Come to think of it, it would be good for our country, too, if we train our bright children well to be part of the new, shining, gleaming, glistening, or whatever you like to call the globalized India.

But then, it looks like you have stopped building universities. Are there ten lakh top college seats in the country? Are there even one lakh? Ever wondered what happens to the rest of us, year after year? Do we join a second-rung college? A deemed university? A distance-learning programme? Get a degree in an expensive, racist country? Your government runs a lot of things. You run an airline that never makes money. You run hotels. You want to be involved in making basic stuff like steel and aluminum which can easily be made by more efficient players. However, in something as important as shaping the young generation, you have stepped back. You have stopped making new universities. Why?

You have all the land you want, teachers love to get a government job, education funds are never questioned. Still, why? Why don't we have new, A-grade universities in every state capital, for instance?

Oh well, sorry. I am overreacting. If only I had not done that calculation error in my math paper, I'd be fine. In fact, I am one of the lucky ones. In four years, the number of candidates will double. So then we will have a college that only has 99 per cent scorers.

My parents were a bit deluded about my abilities, and I do feel bad for them. I didn't have a girlfriend or too many friends, as people who want to get into a good college are not supposed to have a life. If only

I'd known that slogging for twelve years would not amount to much, I'd have had more fun.

Apart from that, do well, and say hello to the PM who, as I understand, used to teach in a college.

Yours truly,
Gautam
(Poor student)

I took a printout of the letter and kept it in my pocket. I decided to do the act the next morning. I woke up as the maid switched off the fan to sweep the room. She came inside and brought a box of sweets. A fifty-year-old woman, she had served us for over ten years.

'What happened?' I said as she gave me the box. It had kaju-barfi from one of the more expensive shops in the city. The maid had spent a week's salary distributing sweets to anyone known to her.

'My son passed class XII,' she said as she started her work.

'How much did he score?' I said, still rubbing my eyes.

'42 per cent. He passed English too,' she said as her face beamed with pride.

'What will he do now?' I said.

'I don't know. Maybe his own business, he can repair mobile phones,' she said.

I went to the bathroom for a shower. I realized the

newspaper would have come outside. I ran out of the bathroom. I picked up the newspaper from the entrance floor. I took out the admissions supplement, crumpled it and threw it in the dustbin kept outside the house. I came back inside the house and went back into the shower.

I left the house at midday. I took the metro to Chandni Chowk and asked my way to the industrial chemicals market. Even though I had left science after class X, I knew that certain chemicals like copper sulphate or ammonium nitrate could kill you. I bought a pack of both compounds. As I passed through the lanes of Chandni Chowk, I passed a tiny, hundred-square-feet jalebi shop. It was doing brisk business. I thought my last meal had to be delicious. I went to the counter and took a quarter kilo of jalebis.

I took my plate and sat on one of the two rickety benches placed outside the shop.

A Muslim couple with a four-year-old boy came and sat on the next bench. The mother fed the boy jalebi and kissed him after each bite. It reminded me of my childhood and my parents, when they used to love me unconditionally and marks didn't exist. I saw the box of ammonium nitrate and tears welled up in my eyes. I couldn't eat the jalebis. I came back home. I wondered if I should use my chemicals before or after dinner. Maybe it is better after everyone has slept, I thought.

We sat at the dinner table. Dad had told Mom not to cook as he'd brought Chinese takeaway for us. Mom brought the soya sauce, chilli oil and the vinegar with cut green chillies in little katoris. We ate American chopsuey on stainless steel plates. I looked at my watch, it was 8 p.m. Three more hours, I thought as I let out a sigh.

'One thing, Kalpana,' my father said to my mother, 'job candidates aren't what they used to be these days. I interviewed new trainees today, disappointing.'

'Why, what happened?' my mother said.

'Like this boy from Stephen's, very bright kid. But only when it came to his subjects.'

'Really?' my mother said.

'Yeah, but I asked him a different question. I said how would you go about creating a tea-shop chain like the coffee-shop chains, and he went blank,' my father said, an inch of noodle hanging from his mouth. My mother removed it from his face.

'And then some kid from SRCC. He'd topped his college. But you should have seen his arrogance. Even before the interview starts, he says, "I hope at the end of our meeting, you will be able to tell me why I should join Tata Tea and not another company." Can you imagine? I am twice his age.'

I could tell my father was upset.

'If you ask me,' my father continued, 'the best candidate was a boy from Bhopal. Sure, he didn't get into a top college. But he was an 80 per center. And he said, "I want to learn. And I want to show that you don't need a branded college to do well in life. Good people do well anywhere." What a kid. Thank God we'd shortlisted him in the first place.'

'Did he get the job?' I said.

'Yes. Companies need good workers, not posh certificates. And we are having a meeting to discuss our shortlisting criteria again. The top colleges are so hard to get into, only tunnel-vision people are being selected.'

'Then why are you asking him to join Stephen's or SRCC?' my mother said.

My father kept quiet. He spoke after a pause. 'Actually, after today, I'd say don't just go by the name. Study the college, figure out their dedication and make sure they don't create arrogant nerds. Then, whatever the brand, you will be fine. The world needs good people.'

I looked at my parents as they continued to talk. Excuse me, but I have a plan to execute here. And now you are confusing me, I thought. 'So should I find out as out some more colleges and take a decision after that?' I said.

'Yes, of course. No need for herd mentality. Kalpana, you should have seen this boy from Bhopal.'

Post-dinner, my parents watched TV in the living room while eating fruits. I retreated to my room. I sat on my desk wondering what to do next. The landline phone rang in my parents' room. I went inside and picked it up.

'Hello, Gautam?' the voice on the other side said.

It was my father's colleague from work. 'Hello, Yash uncle,' I said.

'Hi,' he said, 'congratulations on your boards.'

'Thanks, Uncle,' I said. 'Dad is in the living room finishing dinner, should I call him?'

'Dinner? Oh, don't disturb him. Just tell him his mobile is with me. It is safe. We were on a field trip today. He left it in my car.'

'Field trip? For interviews?' I said.

'What interviews? No, we just went to the Chandigarh office,' he said.

I wished him good night and hung up the phone. I switched on the bedside lamp in my parents' room. Confused, I sat down on my father's bed, wondering what to do next. To make space, I moved his pillow. Under the pillow lay a crumpled newspaper. I picked it up. It was the same admissions supplement I had tossed in the bin this morning. My father had circled the cut-offs table.

I left the newspaper there and went to the living room. My father was arguing with my mother over the choice of channels. I looked at my father. He smiled at me and offered me watermelon. I declined.

I went back to my room. I picked up the chemical boxes and took them to the toilet. I opened both boxes and poured out the contents in the toilet commode. One press, and everything, everything flushed out.

'Gautam,' my mother knocked on the door, 'I forgot to tell you. Gupta aunty came again. Can you teach her daughter?'

'Maybe,' I said as I came out of the toilet. 'By the way, is she pretty?'

My Great Indian Dream

In the United States, there is a term called the 'Great American Dream'. In some ways, it is the national ethos and ideal of that country. According to American author and historian James Truslow Adams, the Great American Dream is that 'life should be better and richer and fuller for everyone, with opportunity for each according to ability or achievement'. The American dream says that everyone has a right to prosper and succeed through hard work, innovation and excellence.

We do not have an equivalent Great Indian Dream. And I don't think we can copy-paste the American dream for ourselves. So right now, what we need is to define the Great Indian Dream. I think what the Great Indian Dream should be is that every citizen should work hard, prosper and succeed through innovation and hard work and once successful, every citizen should give back to the society that made her or him what he or she is. I have been successful far beyond what I have deserved, but I don't think that alone is enough for me to say that I have lived the Indian dream. Until I give something back, I will never feel mine has been a complete life.

These essays are part of my quest to give back to my country. I know these essays are by no means perfect; they can at times be too simple or idealistic. They sometimes, unknowingly, miss out on some issues. I am often not an expert on what I am writing on, and I am only giving an opinion. But what I think is of the greatest importance is that all of us should have solutions and opinions on the issues that affect us all.

And what I want from you, now that you have read this book, is to share your views and discuss the various issues I have raised. You may not always agree with me but what is most important is to have a view or an opinion. All of us need to engage with the issues involving our country. We need to not ignore politics because we feel nothing will ever be done. Things do change and so will our country. However, it will change much faster if *you* come on board. It will change for the better if *you* want to change. Let us contribute to this new direction India needs to move in. When people look back at our times, they may say this was a period of great turmoil. But let them not stay it was the time when people sat around and did nothing to make things better. Just like the freedom fighters who made such sacrifices for us, let us also join hands to make India a better place. There is no Hindu

India or Muslim India. There is no Punjabi India or Tamil India. There is no upper caste India or lower caste India. There is not even a Congress India or a BJP India. There is just one India, our country, which we all want to become a better place. We want a nation that is rich, respected and has a good place in world. We want a society with good values. And as long as we are on the same page for that, I will continue to have high hopes from my country.

Thank you for sharing my Great Indian Dream. I hope that from now on, you will make it yours too.